ARTS, CULTURE, AND BLINDNESS

ARTS, CULTURE, AND BLINDNESS

A Study of Blind Students in the Visual Arts

Simon Hayhoe

<teneo> // press

YOUNGSTOWN, NEW YORK

Copyright 2008 Simon Hayhoe.
ISBN: 978-1-934844-07-6
All rights reserved.
Printed in the United States of America.

No part of this publication may be reproduced, stored in or introduced into a retrieval system, or transmitted, in any form, or by any means (electronic, mechanical, photocopying, recording, or otherwise), without the prior permission of the publisher.

Requests for permission should be directed to:
permissions@teneopress.com, or mailed to:
Teneo Press
PO Box 349
Youngstown, New York 14174

*For the Hayhoe, Pollard, and Manoli families,
past and present,
for being around during all of this*

TABLE OF CONTENTS

Table	xi
Acknowledgments	xiii

Section I:
Introduction and Background — 1

Chapter 1: Introduction — 3
   Introduction — 3
   The Hypothesis and Questions — 5
   The Story of the Book — 6
      The Early Hypotheses — 6
   The Reshaping of the Study — 10
      The Inversion of the Original Study — 13
      The Design of the New Study — 14

Chapter 2: The Social and Cultural Study of Blindness and Disability — 17
   Introduction — 17
   The Social Conception of Disability
      and Blindness in Academic Studies — 24
      Subjective and Objective Disability — 25
      The Application of Objective Disability — 30
   Micro and Macro Disability — 31
      The Micro Theory of Disability — 31
      The Macro Theory of Disability — 34
   The Concept of Exclusion in Modern
      Disability Theories — 38

Section II: A Study of Visual Arts Education and Blind Adults — 45

Chapter 3: Past Experiences of Adult Students — 47
Introduction — 47
Hugo, the Braille Pianist — 49
Sharon, the Sculptor Who Was Afraid of Clay — 55
Pierre, the Painter Who Thought in Colours — 59
Attitudes and Their Consequences — 63
    Rhetoric and Reality — 68

Chapter 4: Confine Negotiation and Self-Confidence in Blind Adult Students — 71
Introduction — 71
Tea and Soapstone: Leicester, January 12, 1994 — 73
    Coffee With the Students and Kate — 76
    Linda Creating Her Sculpture — 78
    Kate Instructing Linda — 80
    Naomi and Other Visitors — 82
    The Difference Between Rhetoric and Behaviour During the Lesson — 84
Sun and Shakespeare: Bristol, July 13, 1994 — 86
    Yves' Time in Bristol — 86
    Entering the Red Lodge — 90
    Exploring the Lodge's Main Room — 91
    Student Discussions in the Main Room of the Lodge — 93
    Yves Is Led Into the Garden of the Lodge — 96
    Reexploring the Lodge — 98
Rhetoric and Behaviour During the Lesson — 100
Conclusion — 101

Section III:
A Study of Visual Arts in Schools for the Blind   105

Chapter 5: Blind Children and Visual Art: Risk Taking, Avoidance, and Negotiation   107

Introduction   107
New College, Worcester: A Background   108
Emile, the Boy Who Loved Lizards   110
    Emile's Educational Background   110
    Emile's Projects   113
    Emile's Behaviour: Avoidance and Denial   115
Anna, the Girl Who Saw in the Dark   120
    Anna's Educational Background   120
    Anna's Projects   123
    Anna's Behaviour: Experimentation and Risk   127
Attitudes and Their Consequences   130

Chapter 6: Art Teachers of the Blind: Understanding the Role of Experiences   137

Introduction   137
The Teachers and Their Educational Backgrounds   139
    The Development of U.S. and English Educational Systems   139
    The Teachers and Their Schools   140
    The Teachers' Practice   142
Experiences of Teaching Art in England and the United States   144
Conclusion   152

Section IV: Addressing the Hypotheses — 155

Chapter 7: Conclusion — 157
    Introduction — 157
    The Book's Hypothesis — 158
    The Book's Questions — 161
    And So, Where Next? — 166

References — 167

Index — 189

TABLE

Table 1. An illustration of Walter Doyle's theory
of ambiguity and risk. 8

ACKNOWLEDGMENTS

Acknowledgments, in particular, go to Rachel Sullivan, John Kennedy, Rebecca Maginnis, Elizabeth Axel, and Nina Levent from my early years of study to present; but also to the staff and students in the unnamed colleges, New College (Worcester), Leicester University, Bristol University for participating in the research; all at Pembroke College (Cambridge University), Maurice Galton, Linda Hargreaves, Ken Fogelman, John M. Hull, David Jenkins, Vanessa Manoli, Chris Arter, Ruth Watts, Oliver Sacks, and the many others for your unfathomable help.

Arts, Culture, and Blindness

Section I

Introduction and Background

CHAPTER 1

INTRODUCTION

> Looking back, you can usually find the moment of the birth of a new era, whereas, when it happened, it was just one day hooked on to the tail of another...
>
> Men do change, and change comes like a little wind that ruffles the curtains at dawn, and it comes like the stealthy perfume of wildflowers hidden in the grass. Change may be announced by a small ache, so you think you're catching a cold. Or you may feel a faint disgust for something you loved yesterday. It may even take the form of a hunger that peanuts will not satisfy.
>
> —John Steinbeck, *Sweet Thursday*

INTRODUCTION

This book explores one of the most powerful myths in modern society: the myth that blind people are incapable of understanding and creating visual arts. In its pages, I explore the case studies of blind adults and children, and interviews with art teachers in schools for the blind. Moreover, this book is the product of an investigation into the changes in scientific and philosophical attitudes that influence the experiences of visual arts and the blind.[1] In addition, it examines theories that can detrimentally affect the self-worth and confidence of blind people.

Through this enquiry, I aim to contribute not only to an understanding of the pedagogy of the visual arts and education, but also to a consideration of the cultural understanding of myths about blindness and disability in contemporary society, and how education is affected by these systems of belief.

Before beginning this undertaking, however, this chapter introduces the reader to the notions, questions, and hypotheses on which this book is based. It also introduces the reader to the structure of this book, the investigation that is presented in the following chapters, and most importantly how this study was first conceived. Thus, it is the objective of this chapter to provide the reader with a foundation on which to understand how this study was developed and can be read.

Evidence gathered for this study indicates that esoteric assumptions about disability have shaped our image of blind people. Consequently, this book investigates a hypothesis and two questions, which address the social nature and representation of disability after the integration of disabled students in mainstream schools. This study will also query how social factors affect the ways in which people who are blind are treated in art education, how schools form their opinions of their students, and ultimately how these institutions manage their roles in an ever-changing social and cultural climate.

The hypothesis and the questions I tackle in this book are now discussed next.

THE HYPOTHESIS AND QUESTIONS

My hypothesis is thus: Attitudes towards students who are blind in the visual arts radically changed after they were integrated into mainstream schools, and this made students educated after this period, in general, more willing to undertake new art tasks. However, where attitudes have negatively affected the experiences of students who are blind in the visual arts, they have also affected their behaviour in art classes.

Accordingly the two questions that arose out of this supposition are the following:

1. Can attitudes towards blindness in art education merely be discussed in terms of a physical disability, or are they affected by social and cultural assumptions?
2. What does blindness stop people from doing in the visual arts?

These questions are not only relevant to the arguments I make in this study, they also address fundamental issues raised by our contemporary approach to disabilities, as visual art education and blindness are always found to be ill-matched. In order to introduce the background to these questions, therefore, it is important to see them through the notion of blindness as a class of *perceptual disability*, and of a broader classification of disability as a whole in the study of education. Thus, I begin by describing the process of its hypothecation and the formulation of the research questions, and the research that is to come in the following chapters, or, as I have referred to it throughout my research, the story of this book.

THE STORY OF THE BOOK

The Early Hypotheses

The research for this book began in 1993, when I embarked on a two-year evaluation of teaching practices in continuing education classes for physically disabled people. During this study, I observed courses run specifically for blind and visually impaired adults in the continuing studies departments of two English colleges: Leicester University and Bristol University. This study was particularly unusual because I chose to observe students who were all blind from birth or blinded in their early childhood, and thus had all attended schools for the blind as children.

My initial evaluation used anthropological research methodology, which consisted of an academic year's observation of lessons (Hayhoe, 1995, 2000, 2005), and interviews with the students after they had finished working or were on a break. After gathering the information, I tested it using the American educational psychologist Walter Doyle's (1979, 1983) theoretical framework of ambiguity and risk. This model was designed to assess the teachers' instructional skills through their delivery of individual tasks to inexperienced students. It seemed particularly applicable to these observations because our students also had no experience in the subject before attending the arts classes.

According to this model, the greater the ambiguities in the tasks given to inexperienced students, the less likely students were to try them, as a result of their lack of self-esteem. In his theory of what he referred to as task management, Doyle (1979)[2] then defined the structure of what different forms of tasks would ultimately produce. These were broken down into two categories: ambiguous and unambiguous tasks. For him, a highly ambiguous task was seen as one that held no firm answer, such as an argument in a debate or the sculptural interpretation of a figure in which the exact form of the goal was highly subjective.

In Doyle's (1979) terms, the amount of risk posed to the inexperienced students' self-esteem in the performance of the task depended upon the amount of knowledge the student was expected to possess. For example, if the task was high risk, then they would be expected to have a broad understanding of the task and produce a highly skilled sculpture or knowledgeable argument after having practised this task many times before. On the other hand, if the student was not expected to perform so highly, then the task posed a low risk, and they needed only to have an opinion in its performance, merely demanding a loose sculpture or a shallow argument, for instance.

In contrast, a task with low ambiguity was described by Doyle (1979) as one that had a very definite goal. In short, it produced an answer or product that was highly objective, such as the performance of a mathematical formula or a technical drawing. According to Doyle, low ambiguity tasks required the use of both memory and routine in their performance, with the higher the risk to the inexperienced student, the more memory and routine being needed for the task. For example, the performance of $E = MC^2$ when given E, M, and C, or the drawing of a spanner of a set size, posed little risk to an inexperienced student, as it only required a small amount of memory and routine (Memory and Routine I). However, the performance of the complex Monte Carlo method's formula, or the drawing of a circuit diagram of a computer motherboard to specific measurements, contained much higher risk, as it required very large amounts of memory and routine (Memory and Routine II). This is illustrated in Table 1.

TABLE 1. An illustration of Walter Doyle's theory of ambiguity and risk.

	High Risk	Low Risk
High Ambiguity	Understanding	Opinion
Low Ambiguity	Memory II	Memory I
	Routine II	Routine I

Reproduced from Hayhoe (2000, p. 241).

In his study of classrooms with young, inexperienced, able-bodied students in the United States, Doyle (1983) observed that the amount of risk to the students' self-esteem governed their performance of these tasks. In particular, he found the greater the ambiguity in a task's performance to an inexperienced student, the more likely they were to flounder and create strategies to avoid it, or the more likely they were to make the task less ambiguous. Thus, he concluded, inexperienced students had low self-esteem.

Similar findings were also observed when the amount of risk increased in a task's performance and the amount of avoidance of the tasks also increased. This evading of risk was especially unfortunate, Doyle felt, as it was precisely these riskier tasks that were likely to help the learning of these inexperienced students most. Thus, he concluded, students could actively avoid tasks if given a situation in the early stages of learning that is too ambiguous, and whose assessment is too harsh. In this situation, students may, he felt, renegotiate or avoid the terms of the assessment to reduce or *manage* the task's ambiguity. My observations based on this theory now follow.

The First Observations of Doyle's Test
As with Doyle (1983), I observed that adult students were less likely to take risks in ambiguous tasks and either tried to

negotiate simpler ones on their terms of reference with their teachers, or even avoided the tasks altogether—they particularly avoided those they had not encountered before. As interesting as this initial observation was, however, I also found that when the students avoided difficult tasks, their teachers were likely to collude in this avoidance. This allowed them to continue using low-risk strategies throughout the classes and to produce only small amounts of work. My analyses of these situations led me to the following conclusions.

Firstly, because the students who were congenitally or early blind had little or no art education when they were young, they were highly inexperienced and had low self-esteem. As a result, they were less willing to take risks in their art classes, even though they were adults, and often avoided tasks or having their worked judged. Secondly, their teachers' attitudes towards this collusion simply reinforced this behaviour, causing a sense of what is termed by many psychologists as *learned helplessness* (Arnold, 1997; Deci & Chandler, 1986), that is, a dependence on their teachers to either do their work for them or allow them to remain unhindered by their lack of progress.

These findings were interesting in themselves; however, for me they did not provide a full or subtle picture of what was really going on in all of the tasks that I was observing for two important reasons. Firstly, in my relatively short study, I was only given the opportunity to observe a single subgroup of blind students at both Leicester and Bristol. Therefore, I could not see beyond their immediate personal and educational histories and test Doyle's (1979) notion that the nature of the lesson task was paramount to their learning. Although I conducted interviews with many of them, these were often restricted to narrow, relatively recent educational experiences within the model. With only a few students did I get a chance to discuss their exclusion from artistic activity at school in more detail.

Secondly, because the study focused on classroom practice and the sample group was limited to students who were born blind or were early blind, the study was necessarily restricted to a medical definition of the students and not a social or cultural one. I did not collect a range of different experiences of turning blind, and thus had no reference point for students who were taught art before, that is, experienced students. In particular, I did not have the opportunity to analyse successful students who had never seen as a comparison.

When I later reanalysed these conclusions, I reformed my hypotheses about the cause and effect of the behaviour I observed. In the end, it was found that Doyle's (1979) framework explained only half of the factors that I wanted to examine. In particular, it focused on a description of the effects of the students' tasks and contained no exploration of the individual differences between all of the students in the classes. This could only be gained through an insight into the students' experiences in art education; that is, I needed a more advanced theory in order to test any emotional, social, and cultural causes of their behaviour in much greater depth. This is now explained as follows.

The Reshaping of the Study

Initially, I felt a form of study that examined all of the students' previous experiences of art education was too complex and skewed to achieve; after all, I was considering a multiplicity of factors randomly colliding with each other. Consequently, I decided to simplify my ambitions radically in order to study just one phenomenon, and eventually focused on the major factor of exclusion from mainstream art tasks that appeared over and again of students' personal histories. In addition, I also looked at how these appeared to affect their levels of self-esteem and their willingness to take risks in the visual arts. Using these foci, I concluded that I could determine their links to significant causes of behaviour when the students were presented with a task.

My decision to identify and analyse exclusion, something I found was a highly negative factor, led me to maintain the notion that there was a social and emotional motivation that largely determined behaviour in the students I observed. Conversely, if I was to identify negative causes of behaviour, I also found positive factors, such as full inclusion in a mainstream curriculum at a younger age that could increase the likelihood of academic success. This allowed me to structure this new study by keeping Doyle's notion of risk taking (Hayhoe, 2002), and adding underlying causes of positive and negative learning experiences. There were two problems, though, that I encountered when considering this option.

The first of these problems was that Doyle's (1979) framework is used mainly as a theoretical model for estimating the success of teaching, and not a diagnostic tool to gauge or measure students' confidence or sense of self-worth. It is also based on the performance of classroom tasks in real time, that is, in a short period of time and in a single environment. It is not a model that lends itself to analysing the social histories of students.

The second problem with Doyle's (1979) theoretical framework is that it does not take into account the emotional factors that students bring to their classes. Students, I felt, did not have to have low academic self-esteem to avoid educational activities. They may have been beaten at home the night before, and their mind was elsewhere. They may have forgotten their pencils and did not want to admit the fact. They may even have been afraid of competing with the better students next to them. They did not have to have low self-esteem to be afraid of being embarrassed by someone with even higher self-esteem than them. In these circumstances, self-esteem and self-confidence was relative.

To account for both of these problems, I adapted and reformulated Doyle's (1979, 1983) original ideas to qualitatively compare behaviour against confidence and self-worth, based on the findings of my first observations. As I concluded from this first study, his observations of inexperienced child students were similar to those of the older, sometimes more experienced students, who would also take fewer risks in ambiguous art tasks. Therefore, quality of experience, that is, whether experiences were good or bad, as well as quantity, experience and age were deemed to be important in my new theoretical model.

By this logic, I also developed the hypothesis that perhaps late blind students, who had been in mainstream classes as children, were relatively more likely to have had positive art education and, therefore, more likely to take more risks. In addition, I also felt that young early and congenitally blind students who had attended art classes in the modern era were therefore more confident and willing to take risks in their tasks in art classes. This highly confident, risk-taking behaviour, I felt, would also be observable in highly ambiguous art tasks.

Therefore, Doyle's (1979) table could be reformulated to diagnose students who were more likely to have relatively high self-esteem, confidence, and self-worth, instead of simply classifying tasks according to ambiguity and risk. Moreover, these students were more likely to have had positive learning experiences prior to their classes. Therefore, it could be said that the culture in which these students had been raised was as important, if not more so, than the status or structure of their classrooms, or even the ambiguity of the tasks they were presented with. What follows is a description of how I reinterpreted the findings that began to question Doyle's notions of the overriding importance of the task of classroom management.

The Inversion of the Original Study
When I began designing my new framework, I felt an inversion of the 1993 study was appropriate to reinterpret the observations I made in this study, and also to formulate a design for a new study. My previous analysis was still too focused on a single set of students in a single educational culture, and this caused a schism in my understanding of what the students were thinking as they entered the classroom, as well as the tasks they were given when they were there.

This realisation was then followed by a more radical rejection of solely psychological and *real time* theoretical models, whereby students were studied almost devoid of any knowledge of their background, and only took account of the evidence that could be gathered and measured as I watched it. Thus, I considered a cultural[3] approach to blindness; that is, I would conduct the study from the perspective of society's attitudes to students' blindness and test the premise that their educational and social culture had affected their willingness to try tasks once they had entered the classroom.

Given this new approach, I was able to conduct an exploration of their personal histories, thus providing a link between their experiences and risk-taking behaviour. Although some elements, such as the choice of students, remained from Doyle's framework, this provided the opportunity to take account of the chances that avoidance can be explained by different, chaotic social and cultural factors hitherto unexplored. This premise was based on the notion that according to Doyle's (1979) theory, although you do not need low academic self-esteem to avoid ambiguous tasks, you do need high academic self-esteem to take risks in them.

Thus, by choosing students with a greater amount of early experience in the second study, instead of inexperienced ones, I was on safer ground. Furthermore, I was also more likely to be able to identify more readily a broader picture of what it was like to be blind. What now follows is my description of how I reorganised the study that followed to explore these new factors.

The Design of the New Study
Art is a highly ambiguous subject when it is studied at a high academic level. In England, at degree and advanced level (A level),[4] students are invited to create and interpret their own works of art from a plethora of different media. On degree courses in visual art subjects, they are often also invited to formulate their own project briefs. Therefore, when I drafted the design of a new study that began in 1999, I felt that I should investigate students who were studying art at this level, as their courses would demand greater risks, particularly in areas where they may have had little or no previous experience. These were the most appropriate students to involve in this study.

To me, this form of study was important for two main reasons. Firstly, it would allow me to study a subject that had previously had little consideration,[5] particularly as my own first study only focused on relatively unchallenging academic lessons without formal examinations. Secondly, by concentrating on lesson observations in my previous fieldwork, I found I focused too much of my time on the *practice* of tasks in art classes and missed much of the motivation derived from studying personal histories alongside it. In retrospect, I feel that this assumption is correct, as the new study's deeper personal and social histories gave it extra depth, validity, and, more importantly, the second time dimension it needed.

Introduction 15

In order to do this type of study, however, I realised that I would have to develop a research framework that would allow me to combine observational fieldwork with these more flavoursome personal histories on an equal level. Here, I turned to the social and cultural study of the classification of disability, and in particular how these notions of disability affect behaviour. This, then, became refined into a study of subjective and objective aspects of disability, and the macro and micro nature of its study.

In the following chapter, I describe this framework. This is followed by three sections in which I apply this structure. Section II (chapters 3 and 4) is a study of arts education and blind adults, and is a reappraisal of my first study through this new framework. The next section (chapters 5 and 6) is a description of my second study of art education in schools for the blind. And finally, section IV (chapter 7) concludes my studies and my application of this new framework by addressing the hypotheses I gave at the beginning of this chapter.

This process now begins with my second chapter, a description of my new framework.

Endnotes

1. In this book, the education of the blind will be used as shorthand to refer to education in schools for the blind and education of students who are blind in mainstream schools.
2. The following explanation of Doyle's table is based on the one in the original study of Hayhoe (1995, 2000).
3. In the context of this study, an epistemological study is defined as a study of knowledge, how it is created and how it evolves. With specific reference to this study, it examines how education has scientifically developed its pedagogical knowledge about the nature of blindness in art education.
4. These are qualifications needed in England, Wales, and Northern Ireland for university entry, and are usually taken at 18. Within the past 3 years, these have changed to A2s, but at the time of my fieldwork, A levels were still in use. Two or three good A levels is the minimum requirement for all bachelor degree course entry.
5. In the course of searching for similar studies, no other similar studies appeared in the significant academic databases.

CHAPTER 2

THE SOCIAL AND CULTURAL STUDY OF BLINDNESS AND DISABILITY

INTRODUCTION

As previously said, the observations made in the first study suggested that esoteric assumptions about disability shape the image of people who are blind. Consequently, the questions presented at the outset of this book necessarily addressed the social and cultural nature, and the representation, of blindness. They also question how these factors affect the ways in which people who are blind are treated in art education. It is arguable that these questions not only are relevant to the arguments made in this book about blindness, but also address fundamental issues, especially the modern approach to disabilities, as art education and blindness appear to be ill-matched.

Consequently, the arguments in this book also examine the social construction of some of the most extreme assumptions in education and disability. In order to introduce the theoretical background to the questions and hypotheses, it is important to see them through traditional notions of the social and cultural philosophy of disability, as well as disability studies. These are both the aims of this chapter. I begin this task by relating my questions to issues of disability and by providing a narrative of my past experiences of these issues.

When I started drafting this model of blindness, I was in a café in Seven Dials, London. One of the other regulars there was an older gentleman, who, I guessed, was well into retirement age, as his hair was mostly grey and he had very wrinkled skin. He lived locally, for I often saw him walking along Charing Cross Road, which was not far away. He also had a trait of shaking uncontrollably. I felt that this was likely to be Parkinson's disease because it affected the whole of his body—the main image of this trait, seeing him in the context that I often did, was that it controlled his ability to eat and drink: his cup had to be raised slowly and not filled too full; the trifle or tiramisu he always ate with his drink was also difficult for him to manage. He had to aim and lift his spoons and cups slowly and very carefully.

I felt at the time that this gentleman found it hard to maintain his appearance as was the norm in that image-conscious part of London. His smell was not what many people expected in the café, and he seldom shaved and appeared to find it difficult to control his beard. Despite this, he looked as though he once considered his image to be important, perhaps the result of a middle class profession; my guess was that he was the kind of person whose clothes and disposition had always been that of a man who knew how to create and maintain a certain type of *cultured* impression.

Consequently, I found the people working there treated him with great respect and reverence. After he ordered, they always brought over his drink and food, even though it was self-service.

I was sure that he suffered pain, because sometimes he covered his eyes and put his head down with a shaking grimace. I also felt that he was embarrassed about his trait, as despite it he was lucid and appeared to be intelligent and sensitive to the other customers. I also guessed that he did not like to be thought of as disabled. I did not know precisely why he came to this café: maybe he was like me and wanted to be surrounded by local people. That would explain why he was drinking coffee there and not at home. He was looking for and reaffirming his sense of identity. This identity was bound up in an able-bodied culture to which it was certain his trait has been a recent intruder.

Back then, his situation reminded me of my experiences with my father when I was young. His trait, though, had the opposite effect to this gentleman's uncontrollable shaking. Dad had inertia, which was caused by a brain tumour. His other slow-growing tumours had started to be diagnosed when I was four. Unfortunately, though, they did not diagnose this one until I was in my teens, when it was the size of a child's ball.

My first experience of Dad's inertia was days before I knew about this tumour. I came home one day and found him standing stock still by the toilet. When I asked him if he was alright, he looked straight through me. He was recuperating after having one of his lungs removed, and so he was still in his pyjamas and dressing gown in the late afternoon. I managed to guide him back to bed with great difficulty. When I found my mother, she said he had been like that several times that day. Not long after, his inertia was joined by photophobia—a fear of light—which resulted in further neurological paralyses and severe visual impairments.

After the diagnosis, Dad immediately got very large, dark glasses that blocked out most of the light from his eyes. In addition, he still was not allowed to be exposed to strong light, which, combined with his glasses and his deteriorating brain function, left him almost completely blind. As a result, I lived in semi-darkness in the rooms he sat in, and this affected our family's movements around the house. There were relapses, however. We once left the fluorescent light on in the kitchen, and when we found Dad in there, he was sitting paralysed on a stool by the door. By this time, he was even more ill, this paralysis was greater, and it took him a great deal of time before he could move again even when we turned the light off.

Despite this, and although Dad slowly became a man we did not recognise, he still did not see himself as disabled. He had not before either, even though he had technically qualified for this status for a while. His only capitulation to any form of disabled culture was his dark glasses and an orange badge for the car, which meant Mum could park it close to the entrances of the hospital or the local shops. For him, though, they were practical objects, not cultural symbols. He certainly did not like being recognised as disabled by others, and so we just referred to him as ill. This sounded like a temporary disposition that would be cured or would kill him. It was not an identity.

Dad's early conditions were soon followed by not being able to walk without support, and he had to use a wheelchair. Like the old gentleman in the café, he really knew he looked different now and was embarrassed by these traits. However, he still wanted to be as socially able as he ever was. I was training to be a farm labourer by the time he had this wheelchair and I was doing a day release course at an agricultural college. When this college had an open day, Dad insisted on coming. During this open day, he was irritable when I had to push his wheelchair over a field. The college, like other farms, was not set up for them. He was also embarrassed when I introduced him to my lecturers and friends. It was against his upbringing to be reliant on his wife and youngest son, as in his mind the reliance should have been the other way around. His depressions became worse as a result.

Had Dad and the old gentleman in the café been born with this condition, they might have felt differently about the help they received. However, they were brought up to have highly dignified lives and to look after their families, not the other way around. They were also brought up in a generation where disabled people mostly accepted their condition and institutionalisation with good grace. In my previous work and research with older students born with disabilities or who became blind early in life, I found many examples of these old-fashioned ideals and particularly met many people who were finding it difficult to integrate into mainstream living when they were older.

Many of the students I interviewed or observed also assumed that they were unlikely to marry, or if they did, they often assumed that they would marry other people with disabilities. They felt they were only able to support themselves through their allowances, and if they had careers, these would mostly involve relatively simple manual work. In particular, many of the people who were blind that I talked with used to be typists or piano tuners; these were careers that people of their generation were expected to take up. Only one student from the group I studied thought he could have a university education. His blindness was ignored at his local school when he was younger, and it was only when it became so extreme that they had no choice but to recognise it. Socially, though, he still relied on help from his family, who adapted around him—although he did not seem at all embarrassed or depressed by the situation.

Furthermore, it seemed as though students who were blind from birth or childhood contrasted greatly in art courses compared with students who developed their blindness at an older age. This latter group of students appeared far more confident and tried new tasks without reservation, and also associated more with the nondisabled people in their studio. Another student who could see but had developed chronic arthritis in middle age also befriended members of staff and me. It seemed that all of the students who had late disabilities appeared to feel more socially and culturally comfortable with people who were able-bodied.

This was not the first such observation of this phenomenon. Case studies by Gregory (1974) and Sacks (1993), although focused on the interplay between perception and cognition, also made similar observations of people who have never had sight but recovered it later on. They discovered that these people also suffered depression when faced with a recovery from blindness. Despite this, many in the medical community felt that it would be good for these subjects to recover their sight and not be attended to during their change to a different, cultural way of thinking.

Consequently, Gregory's (1974) and Sacks' (1993) subjects continued to act as if they were still blind, often turned off their lights so they could sit in darkness, and when they were in light environments, they deliberately kept their eyes closed. They seemed to feign their old ways, and as a result, both authors commented that it was difficult for both students to live in a society where they were expected to behave independently. Sacks also explained that those who knew the man he observed treated him in the way they had when he was blind. This was recorded in his fiancée's journal:

> October 9: Went to church to decorate for wedding. Virgil's vision quite blurry. Not able to distinguish much. It is as though sight has taken a nosedive. Virgil acting 'blind' again...Having me lead him around.
>
> October 11: Virgil's family arrives today. His sight seems to have gone on vacation...It is as though he has gone back to being blind! Family arrived. Couldn't believe he could see. Every time he said he said he could see something they would say, 'Ah, you're just guessing.' They treated him as though he was totally blind—leading him around, giving him anything he wanted...I am very nervous, and Virgil's sight has disappeared...Want to be sure we are doing the right thing [by getting married].
>
> October 12: Wedding day. Virgil very calm. Vision little clearer, but still blurry...Wedding beautiful. Party at Mom's. Virgil surrounded by family. They still cannot accept his sight, he could not see much. Said goodbye to his family tonight. Sight began clearing up right after they left. (Sacks, 1993, p. 130)

As I did, both writers found that it appears it is not just the presence or absence of a medical trait that defines disability. It is also the roles that are defined by the individual's upbringing and culture during their younger years. People who develop their disabilities later in life still often appear to feel the need to mix with people without disabilities. This is their identity. A person's identity as disabled is instilled through social upbringing. "Disability" is *who* they have become, not just what they have become; this is the crux of my study.

This book now turns to a discussion of how traditional medical notions of disability have been discussed in social theory. It is a criticism of these factors that has allowed me to develop the hypotheses featured in the beginning of this book. This is followed by a description of broader disability theories, when I will discuss the notion of the social and cultural construction of disability, and my reasons for criticising the oppression argument of disability theorists. It begins with a critical analysis of relevant studies of philosophical histories and behavioural studies.

The analysis will be taken from two sources. The first of these are mainstream academic disciplines and studies of disability as a topic or a focus of research or broader social theory. In these studies, disabilities are usually subjectified and used to signify general concepts in the broader society. The second of these sources is contemporary disability studies, or studies that treat disability as a separate discipline of study. Although disability studies compares its theory to, and models its discourse on, related disciplines such as gender and ethnic studies, it treats disability as an issue in itself. Notably, it objectifies disability, and the *concept* of disability becomes its focus.

The Social Conception of Disability and Blindness in Academic Studies

I begin my discussion by defining the terms I refer to when discussing the social model of disability: Disability is a description of how a person is excluded from behaving in a comfortable or normal fashion in their society. This is dependent on the era and environment in which they resided. Disability can be visible or invisible. It can also depend on the other social circumstances of the individual, such as their social class or occupation. Medically, it is not an illness. It is the symptom of an illness. Socially, it is regarded as impairment to the functioning of culturally defined tasks.

The social conceptualisation of disability has two further perspectives. Firstly, disability can be defined by the individual

The Social and Cultural Study of Blindness and Disability 25

given particular circumstances: what an individual can do, or feels that he or she can do, in a particular context. This is subjective disability. Although in a social context, this conception of disability is related to the consequences of its medical causes. Secondly, disability can be what a society tells a person they can or cannot do given a particular context and is termed *objective disability*.

This conceptualisation of disability is more closely related to social constrictions and classifications and is particularly noticeable in the sudden change from a disabled identity to a nondisabled identity, such as that which occurred in Gregory's (1974) and Sacks' (1993) case studies, or a nondisabled to disabled identity. The most extreme illustration of this change is described by Merleau-Ponti (2002) in his discussion of the phantom limb. In this instance, patients who had limbs amputated consciously believed they were still present, and this continued some time after their operation. In this way, the new objectively disabled human suffered denial of his or her new condition.

> [The] imaginary limb is often found to retain the position in which the real arm was at the moment of injury: a man wounded in battle can feel the in his phantom arm the shell splinters that lacerated his real one...An emotion, circumstance which recalls those in which the wound was received, creates a phantom limb in subjects who had none. It happens that the imaginary arm is enormous after the operation, but that it subsequently shrinks and is absorbed into the stump as the patient consents to accept his mutilation. (Merleau-Ponti, 2002, p. 88)

Subjective and Objective Disability
In this framework, there are nine conditions that need to be fulfilled for a person to be considered objectively disabled. These are:

1. *The ability to perform tasks unaided in a state that is considered comfortable and normal by the standards of society is impeded by the person's body.* Normal tasks can include driving an uncustomised car or watching television without additional information than that provided by the show.
2. *The association of the person to other people with similar traits.* This can be a person having to admit to himself or herself that they are blind, or coming to terms with the loss of a limb or movement.
3. *The ability to function in comparison to people who are not disabled.* This can be when the person's speed or dexterity is impaired even with assistance.
4. *The ability to look, sound, and smell like the norms that are expected in the society the person lives in.* This can include looking directly at someone when talking in a normally acceptable way.
5. *The person having to use technology that identifies him or her with a group classified as disabled.* This can be a person who is blind walking with a white stick or using a guide dog.
6. *The rarity of a person's trait compared with other disabling traits of similar strength.*
7. *Not being able to change his or her situation.* This can be the difference between being immobile because of an injury or being immobile because of obesity—assuming obesity is not caused by an obsessive condition.
8. *The perceived permanence of the situation.* This can be the difference between sand being thrown in a person's eyes, a person being permanently blinded by an accident, or a person having cataracts that are semipermanent.

The Social and Cultural Study of Blindness and Disability 27

9. *The strength of a person's disability in comparison to the social norms of ability.* This can be the difference between having to wear glasses to read and not being able to see at all. This last condition is itself subjective and depends a great deal on cultural values and conditions.

These conditions can be applied to many social circumstances in daily life. For example, if a person has crippled legs, he or she will be considered objectively disabled. The person will not be able to walk to the local shops without severe discomfort (condition 1). The person can use a wheelchair; however, this would also make him or her less agile or quick on most pavements than people walking normally (condition 2). Whilst walking or in his or her wheelchair, the person will look very different and travel more slowly (conditions 3 and 4), and the wheelchair is also associated by others with crippled legs (condition 5). The person cannot do anything to change his or her crippled legs, even with strengthening exercises (condition 6), and the person's legs will not heal themselves (condition 7). The condition is also rare and extreme enough to be different from a great number of people in society (condition 8).

As it is the focus of this study, the concept of blindness must also be defined in the context of this book. Blindness refers to a range of symptoms that affect the optical information required to fulfil most socially defined tasks. Blindness itself is not a disease; it is the outcome of a disease. It can also have a range of forms and can cause subjective disability; although in many contexts, it can also be considered an objective disability.

For instance, for a person to draw a realistic picture, it is assumed that he or she requires some degree of visual acuity. The person must picture the subject as a whole and must know that he or she is drawing correctly shaped and shaded areas on paper. The individual must have feedback from the lines that are drawn, which allows him or her to know where to put further lines. However, these difficulties can be overcome to a large extent, allowing an artist with no sight to touch. The person can also be educated about what he or she is touching, and be taught to use tactile media such as German film, which rises as soon as it is drawn on with a pen. Blindness in this case is not a subjective disability.

To be considered blind, which is an objective disability, an individual must not be able to perform what society deems as most normal tasks without great assistance (condition 1). For instance, even though people who are blind can read Braille or large print with residual vision, their relative speed of reading is severely restricted. The extra technology needed also requires more storage space, which is less efficiently produced (condition 2). People who are blind often have eyes that appear different, wear glasses, and carry white canes. If they are congenitally or early blind, they also often move their heads when talking (condition 3).

People who are blind often have little chance of reversing their blindness in the short term. If their condition is operable, it usually takes a while for healing to take place, and their sight must also adjust or readjust (condition 4). Many permanent conditions that cause blindness, such as cataracts or glaucoma, can be reversed as a result of diet, exercise, or therapy, but this also takes a long time (condition 5). Furthermore, small visual impairments that require glasses for correction are frequent, yet conditions that do not necessarily lead to normal dysfunction, such as photophobia or achromatism, are more rare and regarded as disabilities (condition 6).

Most societies have formalised their rules of defining blindness as an objective disability. Many Western societies have taken this a stage further and legally classify the level at which this weakness of sight disables most social tasks. In the British Isles, it is felt that only 5% sight, or 1/20 visual acuity, or less (Coakes & Holmes-Sellors, 1992) is enough to be considered to be legally blind. There is a proviso to this condition, however. In the case of traits such as achromatism, visual acuity can increase under low-light conditions (Sacks, 1996), and the testing of this visual acuity must take place in what are considered normal lighting conditions. Therefore, the whole of the person is judged according to a rigid scientific or medical test at a particular point in time, under certain conditions.

Aside from people who have no light recognition, people can have unique visual impairments; this range of symptoms can be classified as: blurred vision, tunnel vision (where peripheral vision is missing), peripheral vision only, spots in vision, achromatism (lack of certain or all colours), or a combination of all these symptoms. It is very rare that anyone is totally blind, and it is much more common to have a small amount of light perception. Psychologically, blindness can also be classified according to the age and type of development, and in doing this I acknowledge Berthold Lowenfeld's (1981) psychological classification of blindness and update it to reflect the early findings of my research (Hayhoe, 2000):

1. *Congenital or early total blindness:* The consequence of congenital blindness or early blindness is that a person will have no visual memory, or the person's visual memory will be based solely on highly restricted light perception, and feel themselves as being fully part of a blind community.

2. *Congenital or early partial blindness:* People who are early blind often have visual memories and can often understand visual reference, but also feel themselves to be part of a blind community because they have been educated or have lived mainly within a blind community.
3. *Late blindness:* Around 70% of all people who are blind in England and Wales are over the age of 75 (Department of Health, 2001), and this figure is increasing as the older population increases. Much of their perceptual and language reference is also still related to vision.

The Application of Objective Disability
In the study of disability by mainstream academia, two theories of the construction of objective disability predominate. The first is that the notion of disability is constructed through microsocial interactions, and that disability is only a reality as a result of the principles on which members of society interact. Studies investigating this theory often have a social psychological or sociological source of reference.

This theory also focuses on the effects of the classification of a person as disabled. In the description of this study, I will call this the micro theory of disability. The second theory is the cultural construction of disability. This theory focuses on the notion that objective disability can be defined by an analysis of its discourse, art, and rhetoric. It also argues that objective disability in this case evolves through myths, which are influenced by religion and the romanticism of disability. In this study, I will call this the macro theory of disability.

The micro and macro theories have many social elements in common. Both agree about the detrimental nature of the classification of disability and believe that classifications of disability exclude people with disabilities. Both agree that society is constructed, to a large extent, around a notion of normality in many roles. They both argue that it is this normality that excludes people who do not fit its definition. They also agree that institutionalisation plays a major role in enforcing the social roles associated with disability. Power is also important to both theories; confinement within asylums and special schools is a tool of power that is used by normal Western society.

Macro theorists, such as Foucault (1989), argued that the imposition of power is total and oppressive. People with disabilities are treated subserviently, have their roles imposed upon them, and are forced to accept their social and cultural position. Micro theorists, such as Goffman (1991), argued that although institutions impose power, adapted behaviour negates its harsher elements. Instead, inmates of what he terms total institutions negotiate order with employees who work in these institutions. Furthermore, Goffman (1990) found that in many instances in mainstream society, people with disabilities collude to form their own disabled identities, and power is not solely top down, and does not have to be defined solely by governments and institutions. This book now discusses this construction of a disabled identity under the headings of the micro and macro theories of disability.

MICRO AND MACRO DISABILITY

The Micro Theory of Disability

Goffman (1990) described the social construction of disabilities in terms of quirks in the fabric of a micro social order. To him, society is constructed through social interactions between individuals in like societies, through behaviour, objects, conversation, and so forth, which can be regarded as symbols by which others define their relative status. Focusing on the extreme effects of social exclusion, disability is seen by society as social deviancy, and the treatment of people with disabilities can be regarded in the same way that social deviants are. These include those such as criminals. Goffman termed this process stigmatisation.

> While the stranger is present before us, evidence can arise of his possessing an attribute that makes him different from others in the category of persons available for him to be, and of a less desirable kind—in the extreme, a person who is quite thoroughly bad, or dangerous, or weak. He is thus reduced in our minds from a whole and unusual person to a tainted, discounted one. Such an attribute is a stigma, especially when its discrediting effect is very extensive; sometimes it is also called a failing, a shortcoming, a handicap. It constitutes a special discrepancy between virtual and actual social identity. (Goffman, 1990, p. 12)

In earlier studies of micro disability, Berthold Lowenfeld (1948), whose framework I introduced earlier, and Vygotsky (1994) focused on the use of social interaction to explain how education socially defines objective disability. Their theories seem less extreme than the purer social position of Goffman (1990), and instead of arguing that disability is a purely symbolic stigma, they break down the context of disability into two stages: the first stage is that symptoms leading to disability are a condition caused by illness, an undeniable medical phenomenon; and the second stage is the way an educational system's interactions unintentionally use categories of symptoms. These disable those who do not fit the expected category of a normal person. More recently, disability theorists have categorised stage two as deficit. In this model, the overt oppression of stigmatisation is swapped for a social quirk, which provides an acceptance of unwritten normality.

A study by Groce (2001) provides evidence to support this micro theoretical viewpoint. She conducted an oral social historical study of deafness on Martha's Vineyard, New England from the late 17th century until the early half of the 20th century. This research was an example of the unique formation of a small, cut-off, inbred community with a rare form of congenital deafness, which originated from a small village in Kent, a rural county that connects with southeast London. Groce's analysis was a survey of the development of this small island community.

Her fieldwork included collecting local documents, which formed family trees, and interviewing the older members of the community. From this, she found that the abnormally large number of people who were deaf on the island actually normalised the social standing of deafness and deaf people. This not only led to an acceptance by the local population, it also normalised bilingualism in spoken and signed English in the description of her study. She found that this unique history played a part in the development of its unique culture.

> [The] trait of deafness was carried by a group of colonists, rather than by an individual or isolated family. For this reason, and because it appeared seemingly at random in the population (since it was recessive), deafness was viewed as something that could happen to any family. In fact, it did appear in most island families at some point. The acceptance of those born deaf might not have been evident if deafness had been less common. (Groce, 2001, pp. 106–107)

This chapter now continues with a discussion of the opposing, macro theories of disability.

The Macro Theory of Disability

Opposing the position of writers such as Goffman (1990), the macro theory of the development of disabilities can be characterised by Foucault's (1989) analysis of mental illness, which he termed madness. The main focus of Foucault's analysis is the rhetoric of literature and historical documentation. Therefore, his works only included literature searches, in which he describes mental illness as a historical construction and a function of power. Religion and governments, he continued, have used the definition of madness to control deviancy. Although Foucault also took an extreme social position, it can also be argued that his case studies show very different approaches. The issues surrounding mental illness are unique, and they relate to more socially constructed elements of disability that change their diagnosis frequently.

In his essay, Foucault (1989) also argued that the social relativism that surrounds mental illness has developed as a result of social changes throughout history. For instance, in the period after the Renaissance, people were confined as a result of poverty in urban environments. Even approaching the latter half of the 20th century, Foucault finds that homosexuality was classified as a mental illness. Thus, he suggests that what is assumed to be deviant, even evil, in one era can be regarded as acceptable, even glorified, in a different era; and as the following excerpt contends, those who are thought to be mad by one generation can be put forward as geniuses in another.

> Ruse the new triumph of madness: the world of thought to measure and justify madness through psychology must justify itself before madness, since in its struggles and agonies it measures itself by the excess of works like those of Nietzsche, of Van Gogh, of Artaud. And nothing in itself, especially not what it can know of madness,

assures the world that it is justified by such works of madness. (Foucault, 1989, p. 274)

Evidence supporting such a framework of objective disability has been used to analyse theories about blindness since the Enlightenment. For instance, Paulson (1987) studied the cultural elevation of blindness in France during the Enlightenment and Romantic periods. Jay (1994) analysed the same in 20th-century French literature. In his works, Paulson found that prior to the age of Enlightenment, people who were blind had been denigrated and cast out of mainstream society; in their original essays, both find that the denigration of sight in French culture was caused by a series of myths, which often glorified the effects of blindness.

The source for this, Paulson (1987) and Jay (1994) suggested, was similar to that of ancient Greek literature. This change in the attitudes of French thinkers occurred at the end of the 18th century. Paulson found that the romantic culture of the Enlightenment in literature and philosophy affected the development of an educational curriculum for people who were blind. These myths then became integrated into education, which glorified the effects of blindness in terms of innocence and moral virtue.

Similarly, Barasch (2001) examined a similar concept in the mythological representation of blindness in Western arts. In his analysis, he focused on the formation of Christian Europe through the Bible and literature of antiquity, and identified a change in the moral allegory of blindness in phases since the Middle Ages, the Renaissance, and the Enlightenment. However, he found that although there is indeed a movement within Western cultures in these eras, there are two themes that reappeared during these periods: The first is the representation of blindness as a mythological punishment, and the second is the image of the blind beggar being subsistent on those who are kind and charitable.

Barasch's (2001) agreement with Paulson (1987) on the place of religion and ancient Greek literature in mythologies of blindness differs distinctly from Foucault's (1989). Both authors believe that there were two strands of mythology: The first is romanticised and charitable, and the second is evil and fiendish. The first strand is expressed more through activities such as giving money, while the second is represented almost entirely through rhetoric. As Barasch said of this phenomenon,

> The simple fact that for many periods the blind lived on alms that individuals gave them shows clearly the continuous existence of compassion as a major factor determining the attitude to the sightless. The other approach conceived of the blind person as a human being who has some mysterious link with a supernatural reality. Most often this supernatural reality was felt as hostile and threatening; the blind, who are somehow linked with it, were therefore perceived as demonic. In rare cases the mysterious reality to which the blind were believed to have access was understood as divine; here the blind [sic] was considered a prophet, one endowed with grace, sometimes with the gift of divination. (Barasch, 2001, p. 147)

A similar view of mythology is again the central theme of Hull's (2001) interpretation of the Bible. However, his is through the focus of a person who is blind and interpreting a world as it is lived and presented to him. In this study, Hull focused on the biblical myths of the creation of blindness, arguing that many of their causes have negative connotations. In particular, he saw blindness as a form of punishment in much theological literature. In addition, Hull judged that the language used in other biblical texts often favours sightedness to symbolise insight.

Hull also argued that the lack of light, and by extension a lack of sight, is often linked in traditional theology with doom, powerlessness, and evil by a great number of passages. This contrasts with lesser instances in which darkness is often linked with calmness and being hallowed, which leads Hull to question why darkness is so often linked with negative causes and consequences by the sighted community, and why there is such a dichotomy of images presented to the world through literature. As he described of these observations in his introduction:

> We read the Bible through the world in which we ourselves are embedded. When I was sighted, I read the Bible as a sighted person because I was embedded in the sighted world. It did not occur to me that I was sighted; I was just a normal person. Then I became blind. After the initial shock and the sense of alienation from my former life and former world, once again I became a normal person. But the Bible seemed to have become abnormal. It came from a strange world—the world of sighted people, which was no longer mine. (Hull, 2001, p. 3)

In this discussion, I have found that mainstream theories have shaped our notions of the more specialist studies of disability theory. This has been admitted by disability theorists themselves, and following the arguments of macro and micro theories this new discipline has moulded itself into a new theoretical framework within the social sciences. In its alignment, it heavily identifies itself with the study of other culturally or minority-based disciplines, such as feminism and Black studies; consequently, many studies of disability have taken it upon themselves to borrow from these paradigms, to link theories, and to use similar terminologies (Barnes & Mercer, 2003). As a result, the study of disability often distances itself from the medical descriptions of disability as a frame of reference but politicises the effects of disability and provides an overtly critical agenda. It is to this form of analysis that this book now turns its attention.

The Concept of Exclusion in Modern Disability Theories

In recent years, disability theorists have attempted to define, classify, and analyse the causes of the medical model of disability. Williams (2001), for instance, took a similar view to Vygotsky (1994). He argued that the body is the traditional focus of *scientific* medical studies, and impairment is caused in the body by illness. This has led traditional studies to focus on disability as a permanent, internal condition, as traditional science sees the body as directly affected by its environment.

Analyses of the effects of disability have therefore treated the individual as deficient and failed to accept the construction of societies themselves as disabling social settings. So how are these notions constructed? According to Williams (2001), the social setting is a form of discourse a person with a disability conducts with a society, which in turn constructs its ideals of normality. Others, such as Gleeson (1999), argued that disability can also be seen as a negotiation with a man-made, physical, geographical environment designed for the normal use of able-bodied humans.

In a reappraisal of this understanding of the nature of disability, Albrecht and Levy (1981) analysed the fabric of such social orders by arguing that disability stigmatises abnormality. Similar to Goffman (1990) and Foucault (1989), they saw the power relationship between the disabled individual and their surrounding society at the heart of their analysis. In one tract, they argued that one of the main functions of institutional education is the method by which cultures deem personal biologically or socially acquired characteristics acceptable and unacceptable, worthy and worthless, strong and weak, intelligent and unintelligent, physically and mentally disabled or mentally able.

Institutions' methods used to assess normality are, therefore, often subjective and differ according to types and levels of institution. It is also argued that social roles are fundamentally defined by those in positions of social and cultural power; these arguments seem to stem from Foucault's (1989) contribution to macro theory. Accordingly in this framework, power is only transmitted from an active progenitor (an oppressor) to a passive recipient (an oppressed person). For instance, Albrecht and Levy (1981) argued that this power imbalance causes definitions of social deviance where none exist.

> We contend that disability definitions are not rationally determined but socially constructed. Despite the objective reality, what becomes a disability is determined by the social meanings individuals attach to particular physical and mental impairments. Certain disabilities become defined as social problems through the successful efforts of powerful groups to market their own self interests. Consequently the so-called 'objective' criteria of disability reflects the biases, self-interests, and moral evaluations of those in a position to influence policy. (Albrecht & Levy, 1981, p. 14)

Albrecht and Levy's (1981) *powerful groups* have been the focus of writing by many other disability theorists too. For writers such as Hahn (1985, 1986), it is governmental institutions and policy makers in national and international organisations that are the main culprits of producing these definitions of disability. He argued that these organisations in particular instigate discriminatory practices and legislation. For others, such as

Oliver (1989), it is the powerbrokers of material culture and capitalism that directly discriminate against people with disabilities. Whilst acknowledging that the government has its part in reinforcing discrimination, he argued that the need for economic production leads to a rejection of people who theoretically hinder it. Consequently, definitions of disability evolve culturally through the self-interest of the greater, able-bodied population. This occurs to further its economic well-being in modern industrial societies.

It is here that theorists such as Oliver (1989) evoke an interpretation of Marxist and neo-Marxist arguments to detail their methods of oppression theory, and a particular target of his is the use of charity and the act of separation through institutions to achieve this aim. Such models of exclusion evoke the use of seemingly innocuous institutions to tacitly subvert people with disabilities. This leads to an acceptance of a lower role in life. Such theories of disability also draw from those of Gramsci's (1971) description of the hegemonic relationship between the working and ruling classes, whose inequality favours the able-bodied over people with disabilities. In theories such as those of French (1994), for instance, power is controlled through institutions by professionals; though unlike Goffman's (1990) theory of negotiation, she saw a more Foucauldian notion. This involves a single direction of power from the oppressor to the oppressed. As she found in her analysis:

> It is an unequal relationship with the professionals holding most of the power. Traditionally professional workers have defined, planned and delivered the services, while disabled people have been passive recipients with little if any opportunity to exercise control. (French, 1994, p. 103)

Similarly, writers such as Kelly (2001) and Fougeyrollas and Beauregard (2001) emphasised the political-economic model of the exclusion of people with disabilities within a framework of capitalism. For these writers, however, oppressive power is created through the historical development of large institutions. They agreed with French that the direction of oppression from the person who is able-bodied to the person with a disability is one way, but their arguments see power being disseminated beyond the individual professional relationships within these institutions and through the sociopolitical struggle of a wider discourse, which exists in the physical environment and economic climate of nations.

Again, they saw the problem of the oppression of people with disabilities in the same light as previous struggles against more traditional forms of oppression. This notion that the discourse about disability is a tool of oppression has been echoed more recently by disability theorists such as Barnes and Mercer (2003). Like other writers, they emphasised the similarity of the struggle of disabled people with the earlier struggles of the feminists and ethnic minority movements, which they sensed were designed to overcome what they felt was *their* oppression by society. In this way, Barnes and Mercer also emulated the language of oppression theory. In their book, they emphasised this point in the following tract:

> Disability demonstrates its own distinctive set of dynamics, although these may on occasion interact with the process of class oppression. Like sexism and racism, [however] disablism expresses itself in exclusionary and oppressive practices at a wide range of levels: interpersonal, institutional, cultural and societal. (Barnes & Mercer, 2003, p. 20)

All of these macro theorists, therefore, argued that there appears to be a tacit belief within the able-bodied population at large that disabled people have lesser human value as well as economic value. This is often reinforced by the notion that disabled people have to rely on charity to live independently, which they find is also the reason why they are all too often educated, employed, or transported separately.

Indeed, many point out that the alternative, older-fashioned phrase denoting disability, handicap, is literally a derivation of a person who needs to go cap in hand for his living, and that this term still recently was influential among many contemporary, globally powerful organisations, including the World Health Organisation (WHO, 1989). They defined *handicap* in terms of the inability of people with disabilities to function in mainstream societies. They did, however, appear to make an effort to tack in a social dimension to this definition—in parentheses they also mentioned social and cultural factors affecting impairments and disabilities. Thus, in their document classifying these terms, they made the following classifications:

> **Handicap:** A disadvantage for a given individual, resulting from an impairment or disability that limits or prevents the fulfilment of a role (depending on age, sex, social and cultural factors) for that individual. (p. 29)

Important as it is in our modern understanding of disability, the WHO's definition was merely part of their three-tier approach to disability that was developed in response to a greater understanding of the need to redefine Western notions of physical disabilities in this and the following decade. More specifically, this definition became refined to delineate handicap from the concepts of disability, which it defined as restriction—or lack—and impairment, and which was defined in terms of loss or abnormality. This latter classification in particular provoked criticism amongst disability theorists for its traditional and authoritarian emphases (Barnes & Mercer, 2003). This emphasis on the consequences of disability has led to what is termed the transaction theory of disability, which regards disability simply in terms of its *stigmatising* trait. For instance, Stangvik (1998) argued that transaction occurs as a result of power inequality and that, coming full circle, disability is thus translated through the two structures described in the following quote, linking macro and micro theories of disability. These bare similarity to Foucault's (1989) analysis of deficiency, as well as Goffman's (1990, 1991) analysis of stigma.

- Disability as deficiency, i.e. the person is perceived as being located on the left tail of a normal distribution of some sort, or lacks ability to complete certain expected social functions. The focus here is the traits and characteristics of the individual. Ability is conceived of as something which can be studied relatively independently of the social setting. This conception is signified by the letters 'dis/de' as in deficiency, disability and defect.
- Disability as 'negotiated social practice', i.e. the problems of the person are regarded as socially constructed and dependent on the dynamics of social interaction. This is no denial of the significance of individual dysfunctions, but the focus is on the social and subjective consequences of these dysfunctions in a particular social setting. Such consequences may be related to quality of life and described as isolation, deprivation, devaluation and repression. Or, dysfunctions may be related directly to psychological and social processes in terms of attribution, dissonance, labelling, social roles, and so on. (Stangvik, 1998, p. 147)

Thus, Stangvik's (1998) framework has dual aspects of power that are the driving force of relationships within disability, and institutions, such as schools and colleges, become those in which power is asserted through policy and practice from able-bodied to disabled people. This model displays parallels to that of Pinnar et al. (2002), who argued that this power relationship also exists between disabilities and different social classes; French (1994), who believed that this transaction of power occurs between teachers who are able-bodied to students who are disabled; and Kelly (2001) and Fougeyrollas and Beauregard (2001), who asserted that this power is also transmitted through the discourse of the curriculum.

It is this analysis of power, therefore, that becomes the focus of my following observational studies. And thus, evidence from the work in the following chapters examines whether such arguments adequately explain the experiences of blind students in art classes or whether more complex social and cultural interactions are at play, and indeed, whether our preconceptions affect this form of education.

I now begin this process by presenting and reinterpreting the observations I made in my study of adult students.

Section II

A Study of Visual Arts Education and Blind Adults

*Note. All of the students and teachers featured in this section have had their names changed to protect their anonymity.

CHAPTER 3

PAST EXPERIENCES OF ADULT STUDENTS

INTRODUCTION

This section of the book examines a study of blind art students and their courses at the universities of Leicester and Bristol in England, from October 1993 until August 1994. These courses were designed for adults who were disabled. During this study, I worked with these students, mingling freely, occasionally taking guide dogs for walks, helping with tea making, and so forth. This allowed me to observe the students working and learning, all of which was interspersed with more aloof observations, collecting student reports, and interviewing.

These methods were all influenced by previous social, educational, and psychological studies based in small, focused environments (Abrahamson, 1983; Atkinson & Hammersley, 1994; Cresswell, 1994; Hayhoe, 1995, 2000; Hitchcock & Hughes, 1989; King, 1984). In this study, I also employed a set of ethical guidelines, adapted from the standards set out in contemporary psychological and sociological literature, which took into account the blindness of the students involved in the research as a potentially sensitive social group (Bower & Gasparis, 1978; Burgess, 1985; Freund, 1969; Hayhoe & Rajab, 2000; Simons, 1989).

My aim in this first study was to examine the previous visual arts experiences of adult students in schools for the blind and determine their ability in class; however, after my observations, these aims broadened into a study of determining whether social and cultural attitudes excluded adult art students or their instructors, and whether there was an observable change in behaviour as a result of these attitudes.

Thus, my eventual objectives for this study were to examine whether there was an observable linkage between experiences in blind adults' visual art education and their personal histories, and to test whether socially and culturally influenced attitudes to blindness and art influenced adult students' behaviour in education, or whether their teaching at the time was more important.

In late 1994 and in 1995, my analysis of this study was carried out in two parts, and this is reflected in the following two chapters. The current chapter describes the interviews and student reports collected, and chapter 4 presents examples of two of the many classes observed as aloof, nonparticipating outsiders. All of the students in this chapter were from the classes at the Leicester University, Richard Attenborough Centre, and they participated in this study throughout the academic year October 1993 through June 1994.

During this year of study, from fall 1993 until summer 1994, the discoveries I made from these reports and interviews caused me to analyse the data in different ways and, through the focus of classroom tasks, make maximum use of each students' biographies. The observations and shorter biographies featured in the next chapter were also collected with students from this course and from the residential course at Bristol University in the summer of 1994.

The investigation was also informed by complimentary studies that I felt were relevant at the time. In particular, I designed a framework that linked learning to the risks that students were willing to take in order to execute tasks, and it was at this point that I decided to critically consider the effectiveness of these courses' aims through a refined, deeper method of analysis. In the second phase of analysis, I applied this theoretical framework to my observations, and what I found was typical, illustrative lessons that I could interpret as narrative descriptions.

What follows now is a presentation of three student biographies, chosen at the time as they represented interesting experiences of the development of the lives of blind people.

HUGO, THE BRAILLE PIANIST

The first student I observed in Leicester was Hugo, a 40-year-old man who was early blind. He had been born prematurely and given too pure a source of oxygen in his incubator, which damaged the nerve between his eye and brain. This oxygen blindness destroyed any vision that he could have developed and gave him brittle bone disease—*osteogenesis imperfecta*.

This led to the underdevelopment of his legs and meant he always needed leg callipers and a wheelchair for mobility. Being blinded in this way was very common at the time of his birth, but since the successful identification of its cause, it has virtually been eradicated. Unfortunately, this combination of disabilities restricted his movement in the classroom twofold: He found it hard to navigate between furniture, and he found it difficult to continually use tools articulately and accurately throughout his lessons.

When he was younger, Hugo attended a segregated residential primary[1] school for children with multiple disabilities, where he was one of many pupils with physical conditions that prevented free movement around the school. This was a barrier to many of his lessons. In terms of the school's curriculum, he told us that during his time there he received no hands-on art education and little music instruction.

The only real memories he had of creative arts tasks were of listening to, and occasionally playing, instrumental music with his family at home, particularly during school holidays, where he was encouraged by his parents to experiment on his own. Unlike his musical background, the only education related to the visual arts or crafts that Hugo remembered from this school was basket weaving, which he found he disliked immensely. In the following excerpt, he describes his musical experiences there:

> I've been a great fan of music all of my life. Ever since I can remember I've wanted to be involved in music, and I was involved in music to a lesser or greater degree. From the time I was very young we used to have a piano at home, as a very small child, and I used to like tinkering around on it. And I remember the first thing I managed to play with just one finger was a melody "On the Street Where You Live" from *My Fair Lady*. And I remember being able to pick the tune out just literally one note, playing just one note, just the tune...And I was always very interested in music. I used to play the mouth organ as well. (Hugo, personal communication, January 1994)

At a slightly later age, Hugo enrolled in a residential school purely for children who were blind or visually impaired, where his lack of physical mobility became a greater issue, and he fell further behind in his education. In this school, although he still had no access to a visual arts education, he was allowed a greater amount of musical education, including his first piano lessons.

However, because of his experiences at primary school and his move to a school where he was more physically disabled than many of his peers, he told me that he lacked the confidence to perform in public. Later in his school career, he also remembered learning to play the recorder with similar social discomfort—although it was also in this class that he met his wife, the student I named Sharon, who is described in the next biography. In the next excerpt, Hugo described one of his memories of this reluctance in his music education:

> I had one or two [piano] lessons [at school], but I could never really seem to…do what they wanted me to do. Probably it was a little reluctance on my part; probably it was a little reluctance to play the things they wanted to teach me. And because of the sort of person I am, and it's still true to this day. I am basically a very shy person. I'm an introvert, I'm not an extrovert at all and I find it difficult to perform to people; and therefore, I suppose because the other people, some of the other people at school were far, far more in a way more competent and confident than me, I suppose I subconsciously decided that perhaps I couldn't actually play the piano, and I couldn't actually do it like they could. Or I suppose I lost heart and lost the desire, shall we say, to play. (Hugo, personal communication, January 1994)

After leaving school, Hugo received training and worked as a telephonist for a short period until, in his early 20s, he became too ill to work any further. He was frequently breaking his bones in even the most innocuous activities. And so it was that for around 10 years of his adult life, he told me, he had no awareness of any form of creative, communal art, whether through local concerts, museums, galleries, colleges, or even instructors, and cared little about what was available either in Leicester or in other parts of the country. However, he did maintain his love of music in this period and did all he could to practice his instrumental skills at home.

In his early 30s, this situation changed rapidly. Firstly, a local society for the blind persuaded him to attend a pottery session at a local school. This was the first time he remembered being able to do anything visually creative, although he admitted that the experience was not stimulating and he did not feel comfortable with their teaching methods. Some short time later, and again through his local society for the blind—through which it seemed that most of the students at the Richard Attenborough Centre were actively recruited, he was invited to attend the Leicester University courses at their inception in the early 1980s. After these initial sessions, he became a regular attendant at the department's studio, often taking fine art sculpture classes twice a week.

Despite this new focus in his arts education, Hugo always kept his love of music and his desire to play, but always left it unexpressed because conventional instruments became too difficult and costly for him to learn privately. He also found that access to this form of education was unavailable for adults with such severe disabilities through mainstream colleges. However, in 1986 he rediscovered playing the piano through a small keyboard owned by a blind friend of him and his wife. This experience is described in the excerpt that follows:

> [In 1986] a friend of ours, she's a girl, she's much younger than us, she's a sort of mid-teens…she'd got one of these little keyboards, one of these little Casios and, of course, technology had moved on in great leaps and bounds over

the years since I started way back at school learning the keyboards. I'd always fancied the idea of having an electric organ. I'd always loved that idea. But of course, back in those days they were vastly expensive and rather bulky. But of course, the age of the small keyboard came around and this friend of ours had actually got one, and she came over to spend the weekend with us and she actually brought it with her and let me play with it. And all of a sudden it was [as if] all of my dreams had come true with this wonderful little box which wasn't very big, with all these wonderful sounds in it, and all these wonderful backings, and rhythms, and accompaniments. It seemed to do nine tenths of the job for you. Well, I was so impressed with this little keyboard she said 'well, I'll tell you what, why don't you borrow it for a few months. I don't use it because I'm at college'...so I jumped at the chance. (Hugo, personal communication, January 1994)

After several years of studying the visual arts at the Richard Attenborough Centre, music lessons were arranged by the sculpture studio's leader, and Hugo was taught Braille music notation by a fellow member of the class—an 80-year-old congenitally blind woman whom I called Cindy—one morning a week. Cindy was trained and had taught the piano all of her working life. Although retired, she took up teaching these lessons as she said she genuinely enjoyed instructing piano playing and performance.

At the time of his interview, Hugo had been learning Braille music notation on the piano in the university's music studio with Cindy for over a year, following exercises set in a textbook provided by the Royal Institute for the Blind. In addition to these lessons, Hugo still learned the piano by ear and Braille with a different music lecturer, which had been arranged for him by a further institute several years earlier. This is described in the following excerpt from his interview:

> [I was paired with] a sighted music teacher…a school teacher, he teaches music, and he agreed to come and help me with my keyboard. And that's how it started. And he taught me. We switched all the automatic stuff off, so I couldn't, I didn't want to play it with all the accompaniment, I wanted to do it for real. So he started to teach me the piano, on the keyboard. And we started very properly. He would record something for me to play, and I would play it. You know, he would actually record it onto tape saying what note he was playing, and demonstrating, and showing me, and saying which finger did what; all this, that, and the other. He still does that now even, to this day; that method. And then I carried on like this and I seemed to be making progress, and then he suggested, well I thought it would be a good idea to try and learn music; to read Braille music. Well there is a publication which is called *Braille Music for Beginners*, which you can get—a Braille publication with a sighted companion volume. It's exactly the same as the Brailled, but it's in print so that a sighted person can read the music as well…This worked reasonably well, but it was all very simple stuff, as you can imagine. (Hugo, personal communication, January 1994)

In the course of the study, Hugo had also just started to learn the drums with a music instructor at his home, which was close to Leicester. He also spent an hour a week having formal music appreciation lessons, in which he listened to and discussed taped music with a lecturer in the Leicester University music studio. On top of all of these separate lessons, he formally practised his book exercises for a morning a week by himself in the music studio.

To pay for these lessons, during the course of his study, Hugo was sponsored by the European Social Fund; this provided him with tuition fees for the charged lessons, a small scholarship, and some expense money. In return, he had to take a form of assessment, which his lecturer agreed should take the form of writing a very simple monthly diary of his activities. However, he did not receive any formal, direct assessment for the performance element of his music lessons.

What now follows is a biography of Hugo's wife, who was also a member of the studio at the time of this study.

Sharon, the Sculptor Who Was Afraid of Clay

The second student I worked with in Leicester was Sharon, a female who was also 40 (she turned 40 in the course of my observations) and was, coincidentally, married to Hugo. Sharon was another oxygen blind baby but, unlike Hugo, had not contracted brittle bone disease or any other form of disability, and so was a great deal more mobile. This also meant she could own a guide dog, allowing her a great deal more physical independence in the studio—where I observed her—and, she told me, around her home town and their house, which had been especially adapted for them both. As a consequence of this greater level of independence, Sharon had always attended segregated schools for blind and visually impaired students as a child, and received relatively little support at home.

Like her husband, she had also not taken any hands-on, fine art subjects at school. The only work with her hands allowed at this time was, again, basket weaving (which seemed to be the stock-in-trade handcraft for most of these schools). During this time, the only truly creative activity she was afforded was learning certain musical instruments, such as the piano. The following is part of her description of this exclusion from these topics:

> I went to school at the age of 5 to Lickey Grange School, which is now closed down. That was near Bromsgrove near Worcestershire...At the age of 11, still at the same

> school, but I moved to live with an auntie and uncle… in Burton-on-Trent, and did the schooling and moving around various houses within the area, until we ended up in New Hall, in South Derbyshire…
>
> There was no painting, no sculpture, no clay. What I do remember is trying to have piano lessons, at which I was a failure…[which was] about [at age] 9 or 10…I don't know. I think I've blocked it out. I didn't enjoy it very much. PE, physical education, was always a part of the curriculum as far as I can remember, even it was only sort of climbing frames, and things like that, and bench-work, and this sort of thing. (Sharon, personal communication, January 1994)

Like Hugo, her creative and handwork activity at this time seemed to be only related to her home life. Here she was given time to work on activities that gave her an expressive outlet and helped her to develop, she told me, some form of burgeoning confidence in her ability to learn. In particular, it was through tasks set by her mother that she had real success. These showed her a different, more unfettered reality than the one she found at her boarding school. The following is a description that she gave of some of these experiences:

> Mum was a nurse and, although she did a lot of shift work, I think she liked me to do things. I was always a very independent little madam. I wanted to do things for myself. And I remember having, I think they were little animal shapes that you actually sewed around. You just did an under and over in little holes around the card with wool or cotton, and it just gave the outline of the animal, or the flower, or the tree. And that was a Christmas present. I remember that very well…
>
> Plastecine I always had. I don't think I was any good at making things with it, but I think it was using the hands

that was the important thing at that stage. I used to want to touch everything for myself. Now according to mum, I can't remember this, but she always used to take me out into the countryside and let me touch things, like leaves and flowers. (Sharon, personal communication, January 1994)

After leaving school, Sharon was given work-related training at an RNIB college for blind and visually impaired adults, and she became a secretary—a post she finished by the time I began our study. As she described of this time,

I started secretarial college. It was then the Royal Normal College, and is now the Royal National College...It was very way out in the country, as all my schools were. Once you were at school you were there!...[I] finished secretarial college, and worked for a couple of years for South Derbyshire County Council, and then got married and moved back to Leicestershire. (Sharon, personal communication, January 1994)

During this time, and similar to her school experiences, Sharon had no formal contact with any form of fine art at all and only experienced music at home. Even when her husband attended pottery sessions at their local school, she refused to go, as she said that she felt afraid of moulding things with her hands—in effect, she was afraid of the clay.

This all changed, however, when Hugo attended the sessions at Leicester University for a couple of years and she considered joining him there to see what they were doing; but it still took time and further persuasion for Sharon to take this to the next stage. It was only when the students at the Leicester studio had an exhibition of their work at the headquarters of the RNIB in London, which Sharon attended, that she thought of practising the fine arts for herself. After this, she joined the sculpture classes at the studio for two mornings a week. This she described in the following excerpt:

> I remember…[Hugo] saying we're taking a coach down to London, to the RNIB, to have a look at the exhibition we've done; Hansel and Gretel and things like that. And I went down to have a look. And I thought, "Goodness me, these are really like what they are supposed to be. They really feel like I imagine them to be. An animal is like an animal." I just didn't expect to appreciate that it could be done, and I felt a little bit jealous in a way. [I thought] "They're doing it and I'm not doing it"… I thought maybe I could do it. (Sharon, personal communication, January 1994)

Since this time—around 10 years ago—Sharon undertook sculpture classes in a group with the other students and, in addition, received the same European Social Fund studentship as her husband to study garden design; although, I later discovered, this funding had not been renewed. During the study, I found that Sharon was working in unassessed sculpture classes for approximately three hours at a time, where she sculpted a clay otter from a stuffed original, modelled a spiral mobile in mixed media, and wove a mixed media design. The clay otter was created while only receiving intermittent teaching from the head of the studio, who was a practising sculptor but an unqualified lecturer.

The spiral mobile was created with a qualified fine artist and adult education lecturer. Both of these projects were instigated by Sharon herself. The final project was created with a qualified fine artist but an unqualified lecturer. In this final piece, the type and design of the artwork was decided by the lecturer herself, as she created this type of art professionally on the loom used in this exercise—although some of the media was chosen by Sharon in discussion with her.

Sharon's work was interesting, as it represented wholly three-dimensional artworks, where touch was not just the primary but the *only* perception used in the design of these works. What now follows is a student I called Pierre, who, despite his early blindness, relied on colour and thus sight as a primary perception in the design of his artworks.

PIERRE, THE PAINTER WHO THOUGHT IN COLOURS

Pierre was an early blind man in his late 60s, who was born in North Wales and spoke, until he lived in England for a protracted period, Welsh as a first language. He contracted glaucoma at the age of 2 and became partially sighted almost immediately. This eye disease is described as

> [a] developmental abnormality of the angle of the anterior chamber which impedes aqueous drainage [intrinsically, water in the eye cannot flow away and so builds up behind the lens]...the eye distends as a result of [this] raised intraocular pressure. (Coakes & Holmes-Sellors, 1992, p. 55)

In effect, he could only see from the centre of his eye, and he could not recognise shapes, such as faces, close-up—only colours—although, he did remember being able to see houses from a distance.

Even though he was only able to see very little, up until the age of 8, Pierre was sent to his local village primary school because his local health visitor thought that if he would have stayed in his village, he may have recovered his sight. At the age of 8, however, his sight had deteriorated to such an extent that he was sent to a lower school for blind and visually impaired children in Birmingham; and then, at the age of 12, he moved to Worcester College, where he lost his sight completely at 13.

He left Worcester College after having successfully completed his public examinations at 18 to go to University of Wales, Aberystwyth, and take a degree in humanities. In all of these schools, he remembered little or no artistic experiences, and the only manual, creative teaching he received was the usual raffia basket work. However, as he described in the following excerpt, he did not find this unusual or unexpected:

> Oh no, I wasn't taught any art [at school]. I mean, the only thing I remember was doing some, some craft work with raffia. I remember that. But I can remember there were some flowers around the classrooms, which I sometimes did notice sometimes, but one of the funny things, and the sad things about going to school were, whereas I remember strongly the look of things back home on the farm, like the look of sunshine on flowers, my visual memories of school were very, you know, very dim indeed. (Pierre, personal communication, March 1994)

Like Hugo and Sharon in our previous biographies, Pierre's main memories of creative activity were his home life, both before going off to school in Birmingham and during his school holidays. Although he had very little sight at the time, he especially remembered the games he used to play, his family's love of music and literature, and his mother's encouragement of his interest in nature. It seemed that these stimuli, more than any others at school, unfettered as they were from preconceptions and assessments, allowed him to develop what could arguably be seen as a creative identity in which he was often able to take risks and develop a unique way of thinking. What follows is an extract about this time away from school:

> I remember having the normal kids' liking for building things. I'd find any old bits lying around. There were

plenty of things on the farm I could make some sort of a wall with...I had a brother who was very keen on music and literature. And I don't really remember a time when he wasn't both singing to me and also telling me the plots of Shakespeare's plays...Well music, I mean people sang at home. I did hear music...As for painting, that wasn't in those days, with the exception of one or two people like Augustus John. That really wasn't part of the Welsh culture. It has become so since: painting and sculpture. It has become very much so part of the arts scene in Wales now...I was never made to do anything...My grandfather was very musical. He used to ride around teaching music.

Leaving home, my strongest colour memory is of having been got by my mother in particular to be interested in flowers. I think that my strongest visual memory was the day that I was sent away to school, which I dreaded, of kneeling down and looking at the bluebells, and smelling them. To me that sort of symbolised, that was, symbolised the, you know, leaving what I sometimes thought of later as the earthly paradise. It wasn't really, it was just a big step. (Pierre, personal communication, March 1994)

After a short while, Pierre left university without gaining his degree—although he later gained a law degree through correspondence. He then trained and became a telephonist in Nottingham at the Ministry of Works, and it was whilst working there that he married and began raising his family. During all of this time, though, he remained unaware of visual arts and crafts, even though he was surrounded by many examples of artworks, and existed in a sighted culture. It was only shortly after his marriage ceremony that he remembered his first real experience of the visual arts. This is described in the next excerpt:

No [when I was younger], I didn't think about sculpture or painting at all...The first experience I can remember

> coming across painting for instance was about 35 years ago, you know, when I'd just got married, and one of the, one of my bridesmaids had a record of flamenco music and, and there was a picture by, there was a reproduction of a painting by Goya on this thing. And I wanted to know what it was like. I think, I think until then I used to go to my in-laws garden, and they had a very large garden, and [my fiancee] used to try and show me the, the shapes of leafs and stuff. I wasn't really terribly interested at that time. But somehow this Goya painting seemed to interest me. Whether it was because the flamenco was exciting, possibly...
>
> As far as sculpture went, I, my first experience of sculpture was going to, was going to an exhibition in Nottingham about thirty years ago, and seeing some work there, and seeing a couple of pieces by Henry Moore. That was my first experience of sculpture. (Pierre, personal communication, March 1994)

After gaining his degree, Pierre went on to work in Nottingham University as a computer programmer, and when I interviewed him, he had not long retired from this post. During this job, he had enrolled in the visual art course at the Leicester University studio when it was originally conceived in 1982, studying on a Saturday. And he sustained this attendance for much of the duration of all of the courses that the Richard Attenborough Centre ran. However, during the period of my study, for various reasons, he had been attending less and less frequently. Of the lessons he had attended, though, he undertook both painting and sculpture, and attended many gallery visits with the rest of the studio class, having some of his art pieces exhibited at some of these shows.

Pierre's experiences, like Sharon's and Hugo's, ultimately raised more questions than they answered in my mind. For me, it was my first experience of understanding what made blind art students blind art students, a first glimpse into how they thought and, more importantly, what made them tick. And in this first image, it became obvious to me that perception was, despite its obvious role in their lives, not the overriding force that many in research (Hayhoe, 2003, 2008) assume that it is. It is this issue that I now address in this chapter.

ATTITUDES AND THEIR CONSEQUENCES

My primary finding from these biographies was that many of the congenitally and early blind students had been denied visual arts in their early school life. This fact was coupled with the observation of these students' lack of self-confidence in both the performance and appreciation of the arts, which was paramount in their course. This issue was governed by two main factors.

Firstly, there was a strong feeling amongst the students that their limited arts education in their early schooling was taught ineffectively. Teachers doubted their ability, which created a fear that they carried into later life. This was despite the earlier developments in schools for the blind and visually impaired, which occurred throughout the middle to late stages of the 20th century (Hayhoe, 1995, 2005, 2008). Secondly, when students had access to arts education in previous adult and community education courses, these failed to reverse these negative influences, did not instil students with a belief in their ability to create or appreciate the arts to any great extent, and *reinforced* those negative influences created at school.

For example, when Hugo described his earliest musical education in the early 1970s, he told me that because some of the other students at the school did not have the mental ability to understand Braille music, his music teachers would almost mentally superimpose this expectation onto all of their students and treat each child as if their multiple disabilities included some elements of mental defection. It was for this reason that, Hugo said, he had developed a phobia for the piano. This issue is discussed in this excerpt from his interview:

> [At school] maybe the teaching I was receiving wasn't very good. They didn't teach Braille music, or anything like that, at any of the schools I was at because the people there weren't capable of learning the, you know. You must realise that I went to schools for the multiply handicapped blind where we had children with all sorts of other disabilities apart from blindness...a real mixed bag of abilities of intelligence and so on...But most of the people there had some sort of behavioural or learning difficulty...so they didn't really teach Braille music, they didn't even seem to teach Braille much. I've had a really strange education really...
>
> I never got the opportunity to learn the piano as I would have liked. And, strange as it may seem, and strange as it may sound, I think initially, until relatively recently, and I mean...within the last...year, I've almost, in a way, been scared of the piano. It's something I wanted to do, and rather than treat the piano as a friend (and that's what you have to do)...I almost thought of it as an enemy. (Hugo, personal communication, January 1994)

Furthermore, of their earlier experiences of adult education, the students would often provide instances of negative lecturers' expectations. In her interview, for example, Sharon described her first experiences of modelling three-dimensional objects. Like Hugo's earlier memories, Sharon also felt that she was given improper instruction by her teachers.

However, unlike Hugo, she felt her fear of learning was a result of the misplaced philanthropy of these earlier courses, rather than a real desire to remove students from arts education as old schools did. This implied that the overly liberal expectations were built into the ethos of these courses, instead of being developed as a more cynical reaction to a small number of negative experiences that her earlier teachers learnt after a period of watching groups of blind students with varying levels of disability. What now follows is a description of her experience of such teaching:

> There were people at the local grammar school in [our local town] who used to do what they laughingly called pottery, and make things. I remember going up there once and being given a lump of clay, and not knowing what on earth to do with it, and given no encouragement whatsoever. It was just simply on the curriculum of the community centre there to give a group of visually handicapped people something to do for a couple of hours on a Thursday afternoon. I was taught nothing and I only went once. I hated it and didn't go again...I actually thought, I am not capable of making things, I do not know how to do it, so if I do not know how to do it, I can't possibly do it, because it was beyond [my] comprehension, and I thought it was beyond my ability as well. I couldn't make the two link at all, so I thought, I won't bother going anymore. (Sharon, personal communication, January 1994)

These findings are not unique. Although they related to all of the elements of the education of blind students, the British educationalist Sarah Dharma Colwell (1993) found similarly low expectations of many students with disabilities in their general school education, in a study of the oral recollections of adults with congenital or early disabilities. For example, in this excerpt from her interview, one early blind student told her about her similar early social experiences from her separate schooling:

> I was a real dudder, because I would never go into a shop on my own. You couldn't get me to go in and ask for a bag of sweets... You've got no freedom, you're not taught how to cope... You weren't taught to find your way about, and how to cook or anything like that. You come out of these places as a dum-dum really. (p. 74)

The literature from the universities of Leicester and Bristol about their courses for blind students highlighted the issue of their need to create self-confidence through learning. Both departments then continued by providing detailed descriptions of their teaching methods and how these were meant to instil confidence and self-esteem. For example, a cash appeal by the Richard Attenborough Centre written around the time of this study stressed the importance of confidence in the students' learning process of the fine arts and the emphasis the centre placed on teaching methods designed to undo any damage it assumed had been caused by earlier teaching. This approach by the Leicester department placed the students' cooperation with their teachers at the very centre of their teaching strategy.

In addition, the statement also seemed to stress a presumed emotional equality between both the teachers and students, thus placing them on what could arguably be seen as an almost equal social footing with what seemed to be equal power. What follows is an excerpt that illustrates this point.

> The relationships of confidence and mutual trust between teacher and student form a close bond. Because our students are disabled and the programme innovative, new skills have to be learned and attitudes modified... Teaching is never one-way traffic. Especially not at the Centre. We

have to re-think basic terms of reference. We must not take anything for granted but question established concepts in the light of our students' experiences...Adults who have never held a pencil—because nobody can see why—can transfer their ideas and perceived images to paper. They can possess and communicate a sense of colour, and articulate its power and use. (P. Williams, 1994)

In the same appeal's foreword, Lord Attenborough described what he saw as the success of these teaching methods when he originally visited the Centre.

I saw people who were blind confidently painting the most wonderful pictures and expertly shaping clay into exciting sculptures. And, although they could no longer see them or had never seen them, those same people, young and old, were talking passionately and knowledgeably about colour, movement and form. (Attenborough, as cited in P. Williams, 1994)

Similarly, in its literature, the Bristol department stressed its commitment to the development of self-esteem in its students, although their teaching methods contrasted in their method of delivery with those in Leicester. Whereas the statement of the Leicester department saw the cooperation between, and approximate equality of, the students and teachers as paramount, the Bristol department emphasised the challenge it placed on its students to perform as sighted students might do.

In their literature, it seemed that the students in Bristol were given little quarter in their teaching appraisal, and there were only qualitative, technical differences between their modified teaching methods and those of sighted students—although in the same literature they often mentioned that these teaching methods often allowed for additional time to experience different concepts, and the provision of guides to each student to help with any physical functions that they could not undertake themselves.

In one excerpt from a paper by the course leader, for instance, Wickham (1998) emphasised that

> [the] courses that we run challenge both the students and the tutors who have to adapt the content of the presentation of their courses so that the students can have full access to the material. At Bristol we have developed considerable expertise in meeting the special needs of our adults…It has always been our aim to provide students with first hand experiences. This is a unique feature of our courses. Field trips therefore occupy a considerable amount of each residential course. In both the science and arts-based courses, the emphasis is still on practical experience and on the active involvement of the students. Thus, for example, blind students are not merely told how a light microscope works—they are given a microscope and encouraged to discover for themselves how it is constructed and how it functions. This may seem surprising, but we have discovered that blind students particularly value being given the same opportunities and experiences as sighted students. (p. 11)

After reviewing this literature, I compared the experiences of my students with this course literature. This is given next.

Rhetoric and Reality
During my observations, I found many instances that could have potentially posed a risk to the students' confidence and self-esteem because of their fears and inexperience. In the Bristol archaeology course, for example, the students participated in many field trips in which they had to negotiate steep, narrow foot paths, climb over hill forts, and walk down narrow steps

to enter castle dungeons. Although these were structured tasks, they posed a risk to their self-esteem, as they were potentially hazardous for students who could not see and who were also often elderly.

In contrast, although they posed fewer hazards, the tasks in the Leicester sculpture studio were often very ambiguous and so risked the students' self-confidence and self-esteem in different ways. For example, in one instance, students were given a broad brief for their exercises, such as creating a piece of a city using a range of materials. For blind students who had had very little or no previous training in sculpture, this ambiguity would have risked their nonparticipation if they felt uneasy about the task.

After examining the interviews and reports from Bristol and Leicester, I arrived at two questions, which were devised for the more focused and deeper analysis of the observations: When given situations posing high risk to their self-confidence, did the students avoid tasks they felt may pose a risk? And what, if any, tacit negotiations of confines occurred within the lessons, and, if so, what was their discernible success? The issues that were raised by these questions are now addressed in the following chapter.

Endnote

1. Primary schools in England are for students between 5 and 11 years old.

CHAPTER 4

CONFINE NEGOTIATION AND SELF-CONFIDENCE IN BLIND ADULT STUDENTS

INTRODUCTION

In this chapter, I describe two styles of lessons, which I found were typical of the courses at Leicester University and Bristol University. Each was chosen because it represented particular qualities and interesting differences in the philosophies of the two departments, yet shared the common behavioural characteristic of negotiating and enacting a set of tacit confines between the students, their instructors, and those that assisted them.

I term this whole unspecified process confine negotiation, and define it as either any form of behaviour that falls outside of the remit of the stated aims of the course (as I examined at the end of the previous chapter) or going against the aims given verbally, or other forms of explicit instruction by either the teachers or students at the beginning of the lesson. The first description is a sculpture lesson, and the other is a lesson from a Shakespeare appreciation course that included an understanding of the visual art and architecture of the era. These lessons are described through the focus of an individual student in each case: Linda in Leicester and Yves in Bristol.

The original aim of these observations was a simple comparison of the students' behaviour in different contexts and in two different lessons, which demanded two different teaching styles. Similarly, its original objective was to assess the effectiveness of their teaching, using a measurement of self-esteem as a guide to their success. However, after reviewing their content sometime after I had written my original case studies, it seemed more appropriate to look again at these observations with a more critical, or what Geertz (1983) calls an interpretive anthropological, eye.

In particular, I reexamined them through the focus of the social and cultural influences on the students before and during each lesson, as well as how these affected their styles of negotiation with their instructors and their assistants, seeing how more general attitudes to students formed outside the classes affected their self-confidence and behaviour and the ways in which they reacted to different social settings, particularly the introduction of outsiders who were not part of the original confine negotiations. Therefore, I worked to provide a foundation on which I could raise further questions and issues to investigate in the new study. What now follows is the result of this reassessment, beginning with my description of the Leicester class.

TEA AND SOAPSTONE: LEICESTER, JANUARY 12, 1994

This lesson comes from a set of observations at Leicester University in which I focused on a student called Linda, who was in her late 80s and had gradually become blind in late childhood. Although it did not affect her personal history or the physical aspects of her blindness, not long before I began this study, I also discovered that she had started having severe hearing problems brought on by old age and had suffered a stroke that affected her physical strength, mobility, and manual dexterity.

I felt it important to build these latter factors into my descriptions, as they would pose extraneous problems to her sense of self-esteem, self-worth, and thus her confidence whilst I watched her. Above all, I could not dismiss the possibility that my observations of her during this period would also make her particularly self-conscious. And thus, I approached this study with particular sensitivity.

Although she could not tell me the exact period she remembered becoming completely blind, she did remember partially seeing a torpedo during the First World War, just before she lost the last remnants of her sight—this would have been between the ages of 9 and 13. In addition, I could not find out the exact cause of her blindness, as Linda was sensitive about this issue. In terms of her early education, Linda attended The Normal School, Norwood, a college for blind and visually impaired children that was particularly renowned for its music education—an art in which it was thought all blind children could excel (Hayhoe 1995, 2008). She told me that at this school, however, she received no instructions in arts or crafts apart from manual, uncreative cane weaving—this seemed to be the common experience of all of the other students I talked to who had attended this school.

During my study, I did not discover what Linda did after leaving school, as she seemed guarded about this issue too—although, from what I could discern during the year in the studio, she did not seem to have had any form of career structure in her early life. From the little other information I discovered about her, I found that she also had no interest in the fine arts before old age, although she said that she enjoyed listening to and appreciating music a great deal—again, this was an outlet I discovered that was quite typical of blind people of her generation.

Thus, it was not until she attended sculpture classes (first at the Leicester Royal Society for the Blind's day centre and then at the Richard Attenborough Centre after reaching retirement age) that she learnt about the visual arts. She and several other students were recruited from the day centre by the Richard Attenborough Centre and seemed to have a particular bond. Despite this long period of study in latter life, however, I was told that she had never worked towards a qualification in this subject.

During the classes I attended with her, each lasting approximately 3 hours each, Linda only completed a few exercises, the longest running one of which was the sculpting of a piece of soap stone into an art form that was meant to represent a piece of a city. Consequently, the sculpture became more and more unclear during these classes, with Linda and many of the other students seeming to range off into more and more personal subjects.

Eventually Linda's work turned out to be little more than an aesthetically smoothed stone, whilst her teacher, a sculptress in her 60s that I named Kate, circulated around the class—there were usually around 10 students at the classes at any one time—and only intermittently had time to instruct Linda on technical aspects of her work. This teacher to student ratio was much greater than a modern school with similar students, even though the students often had greater physical problems exacerbated by the onset of old age. Also, none of the instructors or their assistants, whose numbers also varied, had special training in this form of education.

The lesson I describe in this period took place in the Richard Attenborough Centre's visual art studio, which was a former kitchen located at the side of the Students' Union building. Although all of the instructions were overseen by Kate, she was helped by two teaching assistants in their thirties, both of whom were practicing artists I called Julia and Michelle, who did jobs such as preparing surfaces for the exercises and distributing tools to the several, distinct groups of students in the studio. These groups, I noted, were not based on the stage of their disability or type of schooling, and those who attended schools for the blind or other disabilities seemed to mix comfortably with those who had studied at mainstream school and became disabled later in life.

The small but distinct social group of students that Linda worked with was known by everyone in the studio as "the ladies", and they were all blind or severely visually impaired and over retirement age. As if to reinforce this assembly, they also sat at the same table when they began their lessons and, generally speaking, participated in the same exercises—although some had far more experience of artistic practice and pursued their own exercises and topics, which they explicitly negotiated with Kate. During my observations of this group, I named the other students Elle, Pamela, Cindy, and Uma.

The exercises they practiced tended to be highly ambiguous, as their interpretation was left mainly to the students' own volition; in this case, the subject of the sculpture was very vague, and the methodology was not set before the students started their creations. The students were also not assessed at all in their performance of the exercises, and so there was no set of right or wrongs in their interpretation of any goals they were set. However, the lack of assessment also gave these activities very little risk, as the quality of the final work was only based on the students' own opinions. Thus, the only confine negotiation they had to undertake with the staff was their description of the piece in discussions, or the presentation, verbal or otherwise, to those outside the studio.

What I now embark on is a description of the beginning of the lesson. At this point, the students have arrived and are sitting around their table, situated near the steps to the door at the head of the studio. This door was raised, and to enter it the students had to walk up outside steps and down the other side into the studio. Those students in wheelchairs had been pushed through a small side entrance, where beer barrels and crates were stored for the student bar above the room. My descriptions begin with an excerpt from my observation notes, in which the confines for the lesson's further negotiations and social exchanges are set.

Coffee With the Students and Kate

> As usual, the ladies are having coffee around the table before they start work. Kate is talking to them about their museum visit last week. Linda laughs, and says "yes" to one of Kate's comments. As she sits and listens to her, she feels a stone in front of her. She listens intensely. As others speak in turn, Linda leans her head towards them.

Confine Negotiation and Self-Confidence 77

> Linda occasionally twitches her nose and her glasses as she feels and listens.
>
> As Kate asks a question, they all reply. Linda replies with them [using similar answers]. She says "yes" as Kate asks them to comment on certain points concerning the sculptures that they had seen at the museum. [This was the Town Hall Museum of Market Harborough where they had visited a display of items about Earth.]
>
> Kate asks them if they can remember the animals displayed. Elle answers, and falters. When Kate tries to jog her memory, Linda nods and says "yes" as Elle picks up the thread [of her answer] again. Uma tells a story relating to a member of her family and an exhibit at the museum, and Linda leans towards her, facing her, as she does this. Similarly, Michelle tells a story along the lines of Uma's. Linda faces Michelle, and laughs at the story with the others—Linda follows the audible laughing of the others. As Kate talks to Pamela, Linda looks in her direction and says "yes" in reply to Kate's questions to her and the others. Again, Linda tends to say "yes" following the others; only by a split second, though. (S. Hayhoe, observation notes, January 12, 1994)

In this initial excerpt, there was little formal academic work taking place. Instead, the students' initial discussions about the visit served a vital social function in the settling of their tacit rules of engagement for the tasks that were to follow, as well as acted as an introduction to their exercises, which lowered their risk. However, even given this confine negotiation, Linda was still reluctant to risk her participation. She did not make independent comments about the visit she had participated in or tell stories like some of her other classmates, and she only replied with the others, or after them, with short, one-word answers. In the event, she did not seem worried as there was no pressure exerted on her or the others to expand on any of their points or comment, and thus she knew she was allowed to sit back and participate in a soft manner.

The episode from this lesson that now follows continues after the ladies have finished their coffee and move onto their sculptures, and again begins with the relevant excerpt from my observation notes.

Linda Creating Her Sculpture

> Linda continues to file with her right hand, holding the stone with her left. She puts down the file she has just used and picks up another, also on the table in front of her. This file has a thin, round blade. Previously, this had been placed next to Linda. To find it, Linda feels around in its approximate area. After feeling the file on the table and picking it up, she feels for its top and handle bottom. She then grips its handle.
>
> After using it for a while, Linda puts the file back down. She now feels behind her for her bag resting on the chair's back, pulls an overall jacket out of it and then tries to put it on. Seeing this, Julia walks around and helps her to put it on as Linda was having a little difficulty in doing so. Linda now picks up her flat file again, and resumes filing her piece of stone. She then lays the stone flat on the table. As she files, Linda starts into conversation with Elle. As Linda continues to file, she picks the stone up and manoeuvres it with one hand—she is now lifting her stone a lot more with her left hand as she files. Periodically, Linda stops filing and lifts and feels her whole stone with both of her hands. She then lays the stone flat again and resumes filing.
>
> Linda picks up the round file in front of her and continues. Again, her left hand moves around and over the stone

as she files with her right; intermittently, Elle continues to talk to Linda next to her. As she does so, Linda turns her head, her ear facing Elle. Linda has quite a few tools scattered around her, all within her easy reaching distance [although she does not use many of them in this class].

Kate comes up to Linda and asks her if she would like a cushion for her stone, Linda says "yes", and Kate fetches one. The stone is placed on top of the cushion, and Linda resumes filing with her large, flat file. Linda continues holding the file with her left hand and files the stone with her right. Linda talks to Elle about her neighbours, and as she does so she slows her filing slightly, takes broader, longer strokes, and grips the stone less with her right hand. Eventually Linda talks to Elle more intensely, and as she does so stops filing the stone altogether. (S. Hayhoe, observation notes, January 12, 1994)

In this second excerpt, I most often noted that Linda continued the work on her sculpture from earlier lessons more comfortably on what was a low-risk activity and only using some of the simple tools placed in her immediate vicinity, as she seemed to know that this form of work would not be challenged by those around her; thus, the indistinctness did not require her work to be of a high standard.

A further observation I made during this episode, was that when left alone and in what became social settings, Linda freely discussed issues with the student next to her, Elle, even prioritising this over her academic work in order to do so. In this excerpt, it was also noticeable that both Linda and Kate went out of their way to make Linda as comfortable as possible as she completed this work, not interrupting her socialising or simple filing strokes, which seemed to provide little challenge to the eventual topic. What now follows is the one-to-one instruction that Kate provided after a short period of Linda's relative inactivity.

Kate Instructing Linda

Kate comes over again, and talks about the tools that Linda is using and then [after a short while] leaves. Linda continues to file on her own, as Elle asks Linda a short question about the tools, and they both continue. Someone else comes into the studio and talks to Kate (we do not recognise her). Linda hears the new woman, and asks Elle who it is. Elle tells her, Linda says something else to her [that is imperceptible] and they continue. Linda continues to file. She asks Elle who is it that is chipping at stone in another part of the studio and Elle replies, saying who she thinks it is. After this break in their work they both discuss a pottery wheel the studio wants to buy, and eventually continue working.

After a short while, Linda stops filing her stone again for a little time, and instead feels its surfaces up and down. Michelle [the class assistant] then comes over and talks to Linda for a while. Linda stops filing as she does this, and bends her head to Michelle so that her ear faces her. As Michelle comments to Linda about her work, Linda repeats the last word of Michelle's sentences and then, after she has finished talking, Linda picks up her file and continues smoothing the work.

[Again a short time afterwards], Linda puts down her file and picks up a brush to clean excess dust from her stone, and then moves it around in her hand a little more, stands and picks it up. She says to Elle, "I'll just give this stone a little wash", and then walks towards the sink. When she comes back to the table she places the stone in front of herself and resumes filing, but this time a great deal quicker than before. Kate comes up again and asks Linda what she is going to do with it. "Filing it smooth?" Without eliciting an answer, Kate tells her that she would do a lot better with a rasp, which she then proceeds to pick up and hands it to Linda handle first. Linda feels for the file in front of her and, after touching it, feels for the handle with her right hand and moves her left hand to the other end of the rasp.

Linda grips its handle and starts to file the stone with Kate holding her hand onto the handle. The stone starts moving as a result of this more vigorous pace, and so Linda frees her left hand to stop it slipping as they work back and forth. After a while, Kate lets go of the rasp and lets Linda files by herself. As she does so, the pace slows from that encouraged by Kate to one more at the rhythm that she had been filing at before. As she recreates her own pace, her left hand seems to grip the stone more comfortably. [Despite this return to the manner in which Linda had always worked, however, we found that Kate did not protest and allowed it to continue.] (S. Hayhoe, observation notes, January 12, 1994)

Looking back on this lesson, I found this excerpt particularly interesting, as it was interspersed with Linda's social interaction with Elle and what appeared to be very soft comments from Michelle about her work. This exemplified the manner in which both the ladies and their teaching staff lived happily within an atmosphere in the class in which the social content of the lesson was as important, if not more so, than the introduction of blind students to visual art lessons. This lack of challenge was particularly apparent a little while after their initial exchanges, when Kate returned to Linda, asked her what she was going to do with her sculpture, and attempted to change the style of her filing by demonstrating hand-to-hand.

As it transpired, Linda was not keen to continue at such a vigorous pace, which seemed physically exhausting, and so she allowed this work to continue for a short while and then reverted to her original activity, knowing that Kate would not remonstrate or correct her for doing so. This Kate did and left to instruct another student in a different part of the studio, after seeing that this method was going to unpick and that it was beyond the class' confines to interfere further. And thus, it was that the ladies accepted what work they felt they could manage at the time, and Kate and the others felt that they had fulfilled their role as teachers in this contented microculture.

My next excerpt from this lesson featured a visit to the studio by a teacher from the music studio at the university, who worked at the centre and occasionally helped out with visitors—I called her Naomi during this study. My description breaks the boundaries of this lesson, however, as it involves a description of a further visit by Naomi and another visitor some time afterwards.

Naomi and Other Visitors

> Linda is interrupted by Naomi and two visitors who talk to her for a while. Linda stops filing as Naomi asks her what she is going to do with her stone. Linda says that she is just "filing the stone smooth". Naomi says that this is "a kind of abstract". (S. Hayhoe, observation notes, January 12, 1994)

During a separate visit, again accompanied by Naomi,

> Naomi comes up to the table and introduces [her] visitors. Linda half turns and says "hello" to them. Kate returns with Linda's stone and [Linda] starts to polish it as it lies flat on the table. Naomi comes over to Linda, and asks her what her piece is. Linda says "it is an abstract". [They ask no more questions after this.] The visitors move on to talk to someone else, and Linda continues polishing her stone.

[As a little time elapses] Linda lifts her stone, and looks in the visitors' general direction. She works at her own steady pace again, holding the stone in front of her. (S. Hayhoe, observation notes, March 7, 1994)

This excerpt from the observations was of importance, particularly when I reread it in its spliced form, as it showed that Linda relied on her teachers not only for physical support, but also as a form of emotional buffer. They helped her to select acceptable behaviour in front of external visitors (who had never been part of the confine negotiations) that she could reuse when she was quizzed about her work in very public, and therefore risky, situations.

Such negotiation worked in a similar manner as the consensual behaviour and lack of challenge that I described in the last excerpt. In this episode, however, Linda showed that this support went beyond the boundaries of her individual lessons and that a long-term relationship was developed over a protracted period of time, providing security in her environment of which she could be reassured before she even entered the studio.

Thus, when Naomi first went over to Linda and posed a question that presented a potentially high risk of embarrassment to both parties, as Naomi's relationship with these students was under scrutiny, both reacted to the situation using a tacit approach. In particular, in this excerpt, Linda took Kate's potentially dangerous question from a previous encounter, "file it smooth?", and carefully reworked it into an answer for Naomi in front of outside guests to explain the purpose of her work.

Realising Linda's initial answer was tentative, Naomi presented her with what could later be used as a fuller explanation, saying it was "a kind of abstract". And so it was that in the later visit with different guests, Linda recalled Naomi's earlier answer in front of her, knowing it would be acceptable as she herself had provided it earlier. This was duly accepted by Naomi, and she and the guests moved on, again accepting the negotiated settlement within the unspoken confines in which the studio operated.

The Difference Between Rhetoric and Behaviour During the Lesson

This lesson involved an exercise that was low risk, creating a situation that had little noticeable effect on the creation of Linda's self-confidence. In fact, the ambiguity of the exercise seemed to increase Linda's apathy towards her intellectual performance in class, and the end product turned out to be only an aesthetically smoothed stone. There was also a very distinct partnership between students, teachers, and assistants through which she could rely on the set of rules that had been tacitly established to not threaten her extremely fragile self-confidence, and more importantly, to create a safe environment in which they could continue the charitable work that both groups had come to need and rely upon.

Thus, Linda's behaviour tended towards avoidance and dependence, which contributed little to the indifferent sculpture she eventually produced. This was seen especially in three instances of her behaviour and demonstrated a heightened sense of emotional intelligence in first interpreting their rules and then applying these strategies in the most appropriate context. Firstly, Linda did not initiate any of her own conversations about her sculpture or the museum they visited in a previous session, especially in front of the staff. This was in comparison to her extensive social dialogue with Elle, a seemingly more confident student from the ladies, during the exercise.

Secondly, Linda's academic work was slow and at best noncommittal, even when her performance of the activity was changed by Kate, when she demonstrated a faster, more vigorous way of sculpting her stone. Thirdly, when Linda was confronted by Naomi with a situation in which she was asked to explain her work, in the first lesson Linda gave a very vague answer, to which Naomi presented her with an answer of her own. However, in a following visit by Naomi and other visitors, Linda offered Naomi this same answer.

In response, the teacher and her assistants employed three acceptable strategies to avoid unduly embarrassing Linda or damaging what was an already fragile self-confidence. Firstly, Kate and Michelle only provided Linda with passive comments about her sculpture, which were often very complimentary, although it was obvious that the exercise was not very exciting or challenging to her and her work was fairly lack lustre; indeed, this strategy was far less risky than trying to initiate a discussion with her about her sculpture, in which she took little interest.

Secondly, perhaps not realising this situation, as she was not involved in the teaching, when Naomi attempted to ask Linda about her sculpture in front of visitors on two separate occasions, she quickly left when Linda showed little willingness to embark on a discussion about it, and she realised the situation could become uncomfortable. Thirdly, the nature of the exercise was left unassessed, with the students being given no benchmark to perform to, which posed no threat to Linda. In this case, it seemed that any effort or sculpture was acceptable and praiseworthy, and Linda responded in kind.

Finally, this lesson demonstrated a further element of teachers' conditioning beyond a simple teaching of art. In this studio, teachers' willingness to give their students concessions that would avoid embarrassment taught their students a necessity of a sense of order within the classroom, whilst at the same time providing evidence outside this realm that disabled people were being taught by a powerful local institution, and thus the aims of their charity were being served. Consequently, it also became obvious that this lack of risk was mostly caused by the ambiguousness of the activity, and the lack of criticism or artistic standards allowed Linda's lesson to become more like a social occasion rather than the academic course that was described in the fundraising brochure.

This finding bears a striking resemblance to Goffman's (1990) observations that were described in chapter 2, as well as of Pollard's (1987) theory of a working consensus within a classroom, in which he also found primary school children creating tacit social rules that were not related to their classes' in order to pacify their teachers and fellow pupils. These rules would neatly reduce their teachers' expectations of their performance and, therefore, would reduce the challenge of their academic activities.

What now follows is my description of the exemplar lesson from Bristol University.

Sun and Shakespeare: Bristol, July 13, 1994

Yves' Time in Bristol

In this series of observations, I focused on a student I called Yves, who was his early 30s and totally blind from birth. From early childhood, he had attended segregated boarding schools for the blind and then, after leaving, had trained to become a typist at a vocational college for the blind, run by the RNIB.

Following this course, he found a position with the RNIB in their London headquarters. At no point during this education had he encountered formal visual art education, and so this element of the courses that he usually attended was of little interest to him. His real artistic interests were primarily English literature and drama, and he frequently participated in amateur plays. He also told me that he had a slight interest in music and some forms of nonvisual fine art, although these only remained passing ones.

Yves had attended these Bristol University courses several times before, most of which were Shakespeare related and all of which featured some form of the culture of English literature, and so was familiar with the confine negotiation during the courses, which was relatively informal and made no great academic demands on the students. There were certainly no written examinations or essays, and the only testing of their knowledge was through classroom discussions, which were purely voluntary.

During the Shakespearian appreciation course, he attended four lecture sessions approximately lasting two hours each. The first of these lessons was a recital by two musicians playing Elizabethan instruments; each was an experienced but unqualified musician, teacher, and instructor. The second lesson I observed was a text-reading session, which followed the plot of the week's play, *The Tempest*, and was delivered by a qualified lecturer and experienced tutor for the Open University, who was also the course leader. The third lesson was an Elizabethan cookery lesson, which was presented by an experienced chef and restaurant owner, who was a qualified lecturer. And the fourth lesson was an Elizabethan plant lecture, which was presented by an experienced Shakespearean actress, whose lecturing history I did not find out.

In addition to these lessons, I observed Yves on two field trips, both of which involved art history and the appreciation and theory of architecture during this period. The first was approximately four hours long and the second, two and a half. The first of these trips was a visit to an Elizabethan mansion house and grounds in Somerset, the academic content of which was taught by a qualified historian and writer, who was also accompanied by the course leader and an academic support tutor. The latter of these staff were always there to assist with the students' mobility during the day. The second field visit was to an Elizabethan house called the Red Lodge, in the centre of Bristol. It is the lesson featured in this description.

During this lesson, the students were again accompanied by the course leader, whom I named Claudia, and Yves' guide, a female in her 40s who volunteered for Bristol University. This guide not only provided practical help, but academic information and discussions during these visits, such as descriptions of artworks and furniture. Yves also had a guide dog, which gave him a degree of physical independence. The first part of the lesson, however, was a series of small lectures and demonstrations in which the leader and guide remained uninvolved.

Of these staff members, the guides and external lecturers posed a potential difficulty for Yves, I felt. Because he had developed a relationship with his main lecturer during his previous attendance, he had evolved an idea of the confines that they had negotiated, and ones that he was expected to adhere to during his lessons. He also knew the confines that the more experienced lectures would adhere to; therefore, they posed less risk to his self-confidence.

However, the external lecturers and guides had no such relationship, and some had little experience of blind and visually impaired people at all, and thus the behavioural boundaries that they understood were based on a much broader social understanding of what it was to be a disabled person. This was a particular problem as the level of intellectual discussion, in comparison to the Leicester course, for instance, was a great deal higher.

As it turned out, however, the external lecturers had little direct contact with the students and had little chance to build a relationship with any of them. In addition, Claudia was always in attendance and acted as a go-between between the lecturers and students, fielding discussions herself and chairing the timing of each element of the lesson. As a consequence, any potential harm was avoided, and any tacit rules could be communicated by Claudia. These lecturers, displaying a high degree of emotional intelligence, would quickly understand and neither pursue a particularly hard line of questioning nor challenge the students beyond a level each was happy with.

Thus, it was the guides that presented the most telling cultural relationship during this course. They were a constant presence to the students, whether the course leader was there or not. They were the persons providing the greatest support for, and communication with the students; therefore, theoretically, they had the closest relationship to the students during the whole of the course. On the other hand, despite their role as a trustee to the student, in terms of the confine negotiation that they were an integral part of, they posed the greatest risk to the students. Although they had a formal relationship with the students, they had no prior relationship with them and, in some cases, no experiences of working with disabled people.

Therefore, they were not experienced in such a complex process as the tacit positioning of their roles to the students self-confidence. Interestingly, though, I found that this had little effect on their relationship with the students. In my observation in particular—and this is demonstrated in the lesson I now describe—they seemed to bring a cultural understanding of what I felt was charitable negotiation to the course, and almost instinctively had developed a cultural sense of emotional intelligence that allowed them to hold back from, or collaborate with, a students' avoidance where necessary.

This understanding of the guides was particularly useful in these courses, as the majority of the activities that involved Yves' participation were potentially ambiguous and highly risky to his self-confidence. They often involved the explanation and investigation of visual concepts, such as ornate carvings, furniture, and even paintings, using the visual references on which they were designed, even though Yves would not have access to these visual references himself.

This lesson also involved the conceptualisation of the lodge's garden, which was designed around colourful planting and patterns. The garden was extremely difficult for a congenitally blind person to understand without formal training, which he had not received at school. In addition, the physical demands of exploring a house that had so many steep, winding staircases and narrow corridors posed an extra physical risk, even with the presence of his sighted guide.

This theme is now tackled in the first episode from this lesson, in which the students have just disembarked their bus, have been greeted by their lecturer for the day, and are about to enter the lodge. As always, I begin with the relevant excerpt from my field notes.

Entering the Red Lodge

> Everyone is led into the opened doors of the lodge—even though they open out onto the street level, [these doors] look totally inconspicuous—and then down the stairs from this entrance into the main body of the lodge. Yves is led to the handrail as he descends [by his guide]. After the slow descent down, the students are led through a further passage, then reach more stairs and start to climb them. At first there is no handrail, and so the students are led very closely by their guides. When they reach the handrail, they are led to this.
>
> After this initial trek, the students and guides reach the main core of the Lodge. They are led to a further set of

stairs, grandly rimmed by carved, dark wood. There are paintings hanging on the walls all the way up these stairs as it winds around and up. As they walk up, Yves' guide describes the paintings to him. She also describes the structure and environment of the building. Some of the other guides do the same with their students. Yves remains silent. At the top of the stairs, the students [including Yves] and guides are led into the main room of the lodge house. (S. Hayhoe, observation notes, July 13, 1994)

This excerpt represents a direct challenge to the relationship between Yves and his guide. It also illustrates how he is placed at physical risk almost immediately, having to negotiate his way around the building and into the main room of the Lodge. Furthermore, in terms of a mutual relationship, this task shows his dependence on his guide, who has to lead him closely and takes him to the handrail as he descends or climbs each staircase.

Also, in this excerpt, Yves has his visible surroundings and even oil paintings explained to him by his guide, but does not place himself at risk of embarrassment by answering any of her comments or initiating his own discussion. Straightaway, therefore, there is a hint that the paintings mean little to him, and in not communicating with her on these descriptions, he negotiates immediate confines with her in a tacit manner, showing that he is not willing to engage in discussion or risk his self-confidence.

This theme is explored again in the following episode from the lesson.

Exploring the Lodge's Main Room

The lecturer—the students know him from a previous visit to a similar house—enters the main room, introduces himself, and asks for quiet. He then tells everyone to keep on exploring the room [as they had been before], however, this time he wants everyone to do it on the premise that they will tell him about the room. Yves and other students start exploring, led by their guides. They laugh at the lecturer's comments as they do so. Yves is first led to [feel] the panelling on the wall to his left, and he and his guide discuss the room intensely. As he talks, he looks at her. He also gestures very slightly.

After examining the panelling, Yves' guide asks him if there is anything he wants to examine next. After a short discussion in which she lists the other items in the room she leads him off to some further carved panelling. Again, this is described in detail by his guide as he feels it. Yves is now led to a recess and pillars in one of the walls of the room. His guide lifts his hand and moves it around the form of this part of the room. She guides it around the detail of the carving, slowly and deliberately, and she describes it to him as she does this. He holds onto her tightly at this time.

Yves is now told by his guide that they are going to move to a table. She takes his stick and Yves is led by his arm. He has the table described to him once again and his hand is guided over it. On the prompting of his guide, they now move over to the centre of the room and when standing there she asks him what he would like to see next. She looks around again and tells him what else there is to explore.

After a short while of explaining the other features of the room, Yves' guide asks him if he wants to sit on the floor as other students and guides are doing. He says "yes" and they do so. On the floor, they move closer to a small, distinct group of students and guides [that have gathered on one part of the floor]. Yves is told of their presence by her and responds, turning. Another guide moves next to Yves'. In the meantime, Yves talks to the students next to him. (S. Hayhoe, observation notes, July 13, 1994)

In this excerpt, Yves was involved in an activity led by the lecturer that could have proved both confusing and embarrassing, as he had to guess the function of the room through only his touch sensations and his guide's broad descriptions. He was, thus again, put in a position where he had to consider his guide's emotional judgement about how far she should be able to *push* his knowledge and understanding of his environment, and again renegotiate any confines that need addressing as he does.

In particular, the activity provided a high psychological risk to Yves, as it required a large amount of mapping and physical comprehension of his surroundings. Therefore, when he first started this task, Yves was totally dependent on his guide for direction on the panelling and furniture in the room, as well as on her examination and descriptions of these highly aesthetic, visually appealing works of art and furniture.

As the activity progressed, Yves' guide increasingly gave him a greater choice of things to be examined—although, of course, this list was limited to the guide's personal preference and inflexion. Furthermore, showing sensitivity to these newly established confines, after a thorough investigation of the room, Yves' guide provided him with an opportunity to curtail the academic work and asked him if he would like to sit on the floor as some of the other students were doing. Yves took this chance and sat down, talking to the other students his guide identified, again showing the highly social nature of the work and the reduction of risk in the task, and not using all of the time allowed to complete it.

It is again this lack of risk and the tacit negotiation built around this work that is explored in the following episode from the lesson.

Student Discussions in the Main Room of the Lodge

> The lecturer calls for silence and Claudia reinforces this call. The lecturer invites all of the other students and guides to sit on the floor. He then asks them to shout out

their suggestions. Some of the students reply with their answers. Yves suggests it is an "ornate room". More students continue shouting their comments. They mainly suggest its use was artistic. They also suggest it was owned by a rich merchant.

In the sweltering heat more students sit on the floor as the lecturer continues speaking. Yves remains still on the floor; his legs are to his side and his face is pointing down. As the lecturer talks, he crosses his arms, moves from side to side and uncrosses his arms again to gesture, point and illustrate. As the lecture continues, the students remain silent on the floor. A little while later a student comments about something the lecturer has said. During this dialogue, the lecturer also puts rhetorical questions to the audience. He then asks open questions that call for answers. Some of the students comment on these, and the lecturer then makes remarks on their answers occasionally joking as he does so. A couple of the students laugh at these. Other students comment. Yves remains still.

As the lecture continues, Yves faces up in his sitting position. The lecturer is now answering one of the other student's comments and as he does so gestures with his hands. Yves also faces in the direction of the commenter as he does so. Another student raises his hand to comment. The lecturer recognises this student verbally, and they comment; to which the lecturer replies and then carries on explaining the history and function of the lodge. He makes a further joke and, as before, there is some laughter from the students. [Yves neither talks nor laughs during this whole period.]

The lecturer now reads a quote from a book in the Lodge, and as he comments on the piece, he points to the book from which it came. The room is comparatively small for the amount of people now in it, and the students seem very hot and flustered. Yves shifts about a bit in his position.

The guides seem calmer [than the students]. (S. Hayhoe, observation notes, July 13, 1994)

This excerpt showed very revealing elements of social communication between a lecturer that had not been involved in confine negotiations with the students prior to this lesson, although, as I stated previously, posed less of a risk to the students' confidence because he had little close contact with them. It also highlighted the role of Claudia as an intermediary between Yves and the group in the tacit elements of the discussion, which were beyond the academic elements of the discussion.

Essentially, the lecturer's communication contained two main interactions, which posed different levels of risk to the students. In the first interaction, the students were asked to reply to the activity they were set in the previous excerpt, although they obviously felt no compulsion to answer these questions and points, and no assessment of their answers was given. Thus, after his description of the room, Yves, having judged the lack of risk in the atmosphere, feels comfortable about answering the lecturer with a comment about the structure of the room. His answer, however, is only short and about its aesthetics and not its functions.

In the second, longer interaction, the lecturer talks about the history of the lodge, instigating open questions that demand long answers from the students as he does so. Despite its lack of assessment, this discussion still posed a potential risk to the students in the room, as their very public display of the knowledge they had gleaned from the brief tour, as well as that which they brought with them, could have been under a great deal of scrutiny. As the students did not know the lecturer, there was a guarded atmosphere to the comments they gave and even to the responses to his humour. Although this description provoked comments, answers, and further questions from other students, Yves does not appear confident enough to offer further comments of his own under these circumstances, as these questions rely more upon an existing knowledge and informed opinion of the historical context of the lodge.

It also seemed interesting that Yves and many of the other students became more noticeably restless than their guides in the searing heat as the lecturer's dialogue continued. This seemed to be brought about as they were prone to a loss of concentration because of their lack of independence. This was an element that had not been introduced into their confine negotiation, and thus was not rectified quickly by their guides, who seemed more comfortable with the situation and quite happy to sit there. In such situations, their interest was directed by a sighted world and not centred on their more nonvisual needs, and thus they became dependent on it.

This final theme is now explored in the following episode from the lesson, in which the students were led around the colourful garden of the lodge.

Yves Is Led Into the Garden of the Lodge

> Yves now sits in the garden, in the recess under the steps that lead from the house into the garden. His guide, who was sitting next to him, stands and comes out into the garden. She turns and describes the scenery of the garden to him in detail. [At this time] another guide and student also come into the garden and, standing at the top of the stairs, the new guide explains the scenery to her student, and then they go down the steps and sit in the recess too. The student is sat next to Yves by his guide.
>
> Yves is told the new student is sitting next to him by his guide and Yves and the new student talk, asking him and his guide questions about the garden. Yves' guide now stands and goes out again, goes to a plant and takes a

Confine Negotiation and Self-Confidence

handful of scent from the flowers, then goes back into the recess. She lets Yves and the other student smell this aroma on her hand and describes the plant. They all discuss this.

The guide leaves the recess again, and after she has done so Yves and the other student talk to each other about the house and the smell of the garden. The guide, after going around and finding more scented flowers, returns to the recess with a new smell on her hands, and again they are prompted to smell this scent. They discuss this new smell and described plant at length, in the same way that they had before. (S. Hayhoe, observation notes, July 13, 1994)

This excerpt is again important for providing an illustration of the lack of risk and, indeed, the overtly social nature of the course. After Yves left the rooms featured in the previous excerpts, I discovered that he did not have contact with the lecturer and was able to explore the lodge accompanied only by his guide. This meant that the activities in this and the following excerpts posed much less of a risk of embarrassment to him, as they provided no tasks that stretched his knowledge through particularly challenging discussions.

In addition, because he is presented with the smells of individual flowers rather than their visual appearance, he is in a better position to be able to comment about them with greater confidence. And so it is in this episode that Yves is a lot more willing to discuss these potentially threatening subjects, even though he has little prior knowledge of them. This is because it is a more social setting than a more structured, focused educational setting in which issues are discussed only with extreme caution, but few conclusions are reached.

However, it is also notable that in this excerpt he is again physically dependent on his guide for both descriptions of visual concepts and the plants he encountered. It is at this point in the lesson that the tacit social confines between Yves and his guide are most demonstrably drawn. This close social contact away from the other students allows borders to be established, and Yves to reinforce what he expects as outcomes in this lesson. And it is the application of these confines that I again focus on in the final episode of this lesson. In it, the students have reentered the house and are now exploring its upper floors before reporting back to the lecturer and the main tutor.

Reexploring the Lodge

> After finishing their drinks Yves and his guide talk again, and then Yves' guide leads him out of the recess and garden, and back into the house. After climbing the stairs using the handrail, Yves is led into a further upstairs room, and as they stand in the entrance of it, all of the furniture and ornaments are described to him. He questions his guide about these pieces intimately and then he is led to the fireplace and is guided to feel it. He also has this described to him as he does so. He feels all around its surround, and as he does so his guide describes the use and ornamentation of this fireplace to him in greater depth. Again, [Yves and his guide] discuss these subjects at length.
>
> Yves is now led to a chest of drawers, which is also very ornate and heavily carved. Again, he is guided to feel it while it is described to him. This now provokes quite a discussion about the period and its authors. Yves is then led to another room. As he and his guide stand in its entrance, they again both discuss the room's general environment. He is led to heavily carved and ornate pieces of furniture. Its decorative material is described to him in great detail. Similarities with the curtain are also presented to him as this piece of furniture is described. Yves responds to each of these descriptions by drawing analogies. He is then led

Confine Negotiation and Self-Confidence 99

to other pieces in the room, and as he does so he is led clockwise each time.

Yves is then led to the room's fireplace, which again is very ornate. His guide draws analogies with the previous fireplaces they have discovered, and they have a discussion about these, not only about those in this house but in Montacute [one of their previous visits] as well. His guide then describes the steps leading out of the room, and she asks him if he would like to go upstairs now, to which he replies "yes". As Yves is led to the lodge's upper rooms he does not use the handrail this time. As they ascend the stairs, the scenery inside the house and the paintings are described to him. However, Yves does not respond to or discuss these. After a time his guide's description also involves other decorative ornaments, which do seem of greater interest to him, and he questions her about these. (S. Hayhoe, observation notes, July 13, 1994)

In this final excerpt, the activity has much of its risk reduced, and again a tacit understanding is achieved between the guide and Yves, as he only has to rely upon her descriptions and the ornaments she chooses and yet only feels the need to comment when he feels comfortable doing so. Thus, no assessment or challenge to his opinion is apparent from the academic staff. Furthermore, he is only led to feel the most heavily carved artefacts, mostly the fireplaces, which are easy to determine through touch. Yves appeared unembarrassed in pursuing this activity and responded to these descriptions and demonstrations by discussing them freely with his guide.

In drawing analogies and other comparisons with furniture and artworks he encountered in the other house they visited, and displaying his knowledge of the literature of the era, he felt at home risking his confidence and social standing with his guide, whose opinion of him by now, he realised, he did not have to countenance. However, when he encountered the paintings hanging on the stair wall at which he was at a great social disadvantage to his guide and totally dependent on her knowledge as well as her description, he again avoided any form of discussion and wordlessly moved the topic on to an area he felt more comfortable with. Seeming to realise that this was a problem and outside of their confines, his guide quickly moved to a different subject that he understood and appeared more comfortable with.

RHETORIC AND BEHAVIOUR DURING THE LESSON

It would seem that this lesson failed to challenge Yves' long-term self-confidence or his academic aptitude, despite the belief of the department that it would allow the students to explore concepts and subjects for themselves as sighted students do. These problems were best illustrated by the narrowness of Yves' confine negotiation, which restricted the challenges he allowed from his guide and the lecturers' opportunities to challenge his knowledge and develop his critical faculties, and thus allowed him to avoid embarrassing situations provided by the tasks that were given to him.

And finally, it was also very noticeable that Yves' guide often provided the means by which he could reduce any risk in his behaviour. As Yves was dependent on the guide for a great many of his physical and social interactions, he was also often allowed scope to exchange ambiguous academic tasks with social interactions instead. This helped to develop a working consensus within the lesson, not only with his guide and the lecturers, but also with the other students that he encountered. This aside, of course, it should also be remembered that the ambiguous activities in this lesson posed a high risk to Yves, as they could be seen as physically as well as socially hazardous to him, and their subjects were generally newly encountered.

My observations of his behaviour showed that Yves often negotiated these tasks primarily through strategising his behaviour. Throughout this period, two specific strategies were particularly notable. Firstly, Yves used a *repetition strategy* during his class discussions. For instance, he had the first room they entered described to him by his guide, who also chose the direction and objects of the exploration. In the second episode of this lesson, he used his guide's description of the room as an ornate room in the class' discussion, even though this response was not a true reflection of the question the lecturer had asked—he had wanted to know its use rather than it's aesthetic. Consequently, Yves felt secure when his answer was still accepted and he received no challenge to this misunderstanding.

Secondly, Yves, the staff, and volunteers employed an *avoidance strategy* within their social confines in order to create a comfortable social order within the lesson. This threatened neither the students' nor the staffs' position in the institution. For instance, his guide moved quickly onto a description of other artworks after Yves did not respond to her descriptions of paintings, as these new articles seemed to be more easily understandable to him. Furthermore, Yves' guide sat him in the garden while she collected scents for him to smell, reducing the risk of his exploration of the garden and only providing him with immediately understandable sensations of the flowers with their descriptions.

I now conclude this chapter and raise the fundamental issues from this study that I carried into the next, more telling set of case studies I undertook.

Conclusion

In terms of their academic structure, the Bristol and Leicester lessons created their own paradoxes by trying to achieve the long-term aim of self-confidence in their short life span. Such simple lessons led me to reason that their nature was to produce rhetorical access for disabled people into high-profile, powerful institutions and to be seen to be saying the right thing, as much as they were genuine pedagogical experiments.

One observation in particular supported this hypothesis. Although many of the students had attended these courses in previous years, their guides were always new to them and only had a week to become acquainted with their strengths and weaknesses. Furthermore, it was often the case that the lecturers on both courses had not often, if at all, been trained in the education of blind or visually impaired students before they began teaching. Thus, the confine negotiation that was allowed to take place in both classes necessarily prioritised undemanding, often social aims over a genuine attempt to advance students' learning.

This had a knock-on effect. In both settings, and showing what seemed to be a high degree of emotional intelligence about their situations, the students would attempt to avoid risks and decrease any challenges to their self-confidence, particularly when it focused on issues they had been excluded from previously. They achieved this either by attempting to reduce the expectations of their lecturers in many of the activities that threatened to embarrass them or by avoiding tasks altogether by using different behavioural strategies. In turn, these avoidance strategies often led to dependence strategies by the lecturers and their assistants who presented answers for them and helped them work, thus reducing the risks of tasks. This contributed to a comfortable, noninvasive, unchallenging, and above all nonthreatening social order.

And so it was that this first study raised different issues about students' willingness to learn in art classes, especially those who had no or little experience of this form of education as children. In addition, it showed how they were happy to accept lesser social and cultural worth for themselves, and were allowed to apply this worth during their lessons. In this way, social power was maintained for the institutions and their staff, and a comfortable social order was maintained for the students.

For me, this issue raised questions about the role of confidence and motivation as an aspect of self-worth and, moreover, how a lack of confidence and motivation would affect blind students' learning. Thus, in my following study, I explored these experiences and the aspects of the behaviour of students who had the opportunity to learn art during their childhood, and the worth that resulted from this integration.

Section III

A Study of Visual Arts in Schools for the Blind

*Note. All of the students and teachers featured in this section also have had their names changed to protect their anonymity.

CHAPTER 5

BLIND CHILDREN AND VISUAL ART: RISK TAKING, AVOIDANCE, AND NEGOTIATION

INTRODUCTION

This section of the book considers the experiences of two students who studied visual art at New College, Worcester, and the observations of art teachers in similar schools in the United Kingdom and the United States. In doing so, it develops an examination of the issue I raised at the very end of the previous chapter. In addition, over the next two chapters I also examine the notion that previous experiences have directly affected students' behaviour, and thus tests the hypotheses I presented in the first chapter. It examines whether there is an observable linkage between early experiences of the visual arts and students' later experience of the visual arts, and whether socially and culturally influenced attitudes to blindness can influence later behaviour and social and cultural worth.

This first chapter in the section presents descriptions of these two students as case studies. Both students, a boy and a girl, were registered blind early in their lives, attended a mainstream school in their early years of education, and then attended New College after being referred by their Local Education Authority[1] (LEA). I called the boy Emile and the girl Anna. After these case studies, I then present my conclusions based on my observations of both students combined, just as I did with the lesson analyses in the previous chapter.

Before beginning these case studies, however, I give a brief description of New College, Worcester. This background narrative is designed to provide you, the reader, with the context of the case studies, a surface level understanding of the teaching the students received, and their personal histories against the broader social and political history of the school.

NEW COLLEGE, WORCESTER: A BACKGROUND

The students featured in the following case studies were admitted to New College's upper school, which evolved in the 19th century after the amalgamation of other Royal National Institute for the Blind (RNIB) schools into the original Worcester College, previously called Worcester College for the Blind Sons of Gentlemen (Hayhoe, 2008). The legacy of this original school still exists, as it is a registered charity and its funding comes in the form of fees—mostly from LEAs. The school is also a member of the Headmaster's Conference (HMC).

The school has regular annual student numbers below 100, and all of these students have an official government statement of special educational needs related to their blindness. They are assessed both before arriving at the college by their local authorities, and by the college after they arrive. All of the students live on the campus during term-time weekdays and are supported by live-in help assistants—many of these are college students from the United Kingdom and North America.

New College now teaches students up to 19 years old, although this is not common, as most students leave either in their 16th or 18th year. Class sizes are small, with usually a maximum of five in each lesson. Despite this concentrated attention, however, the school's curriculum is extensive and covers a broad range of humanities, sciences, technologies, sports, and the arts—including fine art, drama, and music. To facilitate this teaching, special resources are available to allow for adapted learning practices, such as large-screen computers and special sports equipment. Consequently, because their educational standards are high, all of the subject departments offer GCSE courses for 14 to 16 year olds, and most offer A-level courses for students from 16 years old onwards.

Geographically, the school buildings are on a single campus on the southern outskirts of Worcester—a small, historical city in the English west midlands, founded during the Roman era—and were built for the purpose of educating students who were blind at the beginning of the 20th century. This campus has large, landscaped grounds with rugged countryside and fields surrounding it. It looks onto the nearby Malvern Hills on one side, and the smartly presented modern and Victorian suburbs of this part of Worcester on the other. The school can be accessed by the nearby motorway and main roads, or the frequent buses that pass close by its entrance and travel into the city centre. This makes the school less isolated than similar institutions, which are often located deep into the countryside, and students are often seen around the town or catching a train home by themselves from Worcester station.

I now describe the experiences of Emile, the first of my case studies.

EMILE, THE BOY WHO LOVED LIZARDS

Emile's Educational Background

Emile[2] was 18 years old when I began my fieldwork at New College, a year older than most students in his year group, and he came from a middle class family that lived in south east England. His blindness was caused by an atrophic condition called congenital optic nerve hyperplasia, which was degenerative, although during this study he still had enough vision to be able to do art tasks such as photography, and could also see pictures if he held them very close to his eyes.

In terms of its medical description, optic nerve conditions are described by Coakes and Holmes Sellors (1988) in terms of three factors: "Disease of the optic nerve or chiasm usually results in:…Decreased visual acuity…Visual field loss…Optic atrophy" (p. 36). Atrophies such as Emile's are also thought to cause either loss of peripheral or central vision, and to reduce colour perception. Emile would, therefore, have only seen blocks of limited amounts of colour with no details. His eyes also appeared to flicker a great deal and could not focus as unaffected eyes do.

Emile began at New College in the earliest year of senior school. He transferred from a mainstream school system after his mother lobbied his local authority for him to change types of school, as she felt that he had suffered segregation within his earlier mainstream classes and that New College would provide better facilities for him. Before going to New College, Emile told me that he usually found himself sidelined in many of his classes, and that his family felt that his teachers did not have the experience or resources to deal with students who were blind or visually impaired.

During my study, I noted that Emile referred a great deal to his negative experiences in early mainstream art classes. He particularly took pains to explain that whilst being taught to draw and copy, he was singled out by his teachers for special treatment. In particular, Emile told me that they often felt he was incapable of using pencils and other such equipment, and did not attempt to assess his work as they did his sighted peers. Eventually, he felt as if he had to attend the art lessons, but his teachers believed he could not get much from them, and this made him feel that he could not get much of these forms of art. The next excerpt, from his diary, gives an illustration of these experiences:

> I had very little art education before I came to Worcester. It mainly consisted of drawing pictures with large felt tip crayons because they thought that I couldn't cope with pencil and pens. I can remember painting and drawing at home whilst at [junior] school because my parents thought that the school was not doing enough to stimulate my artistic side. Between the ages of 11 and 14, I was at the school I am presently at now, and we did do art in lesson time. And for GCSEs we did do art. I did expressive arts [also]...that's near enough the same thing.
> (Emile, personal communication, March 2000)

Unwittingly, during my interview, Emile also let it be known that he had negative experiences of literacy in his earlier mainstream classes. In particular, he had no access to large-print materials, and so could not read effectively. This left him "hating" tasks involving copious amounts of writing, and he found he could barely read when he entered New College. He measured himself against blind and partially sighted peers with access to the proper facilities. Emile said that this was the reason he had to be put back a year in all of his subjects when he first transferred schools, and his art teacher, Gerard, confirmed this in a later interview I held with him.

In terms of his choice of subject, Emile said that he became interested in art after starting at New College, and he especially enjoyed the molding of clay masks and sculpture sessions. He found that he particularly enjoyed the means of self-expression it gave him, and he also appreciated the fact that he did not have to write much in this subject. He subsequently took GCSE art from the age of 14 to 16 and then decided to take A-level fine art. Emile also told me that he began A levels in biology and chemistry in the same period, but abandoned his chemistry course shortly after beginning it. Later in this run of participant observations, he also told me that he was going to abandon his biology course as well. Eventually, art was his only A level.

Later, however, Emile confided that despite abandoning biology, he still had a passion for the subject and felt as though he also had an affinity with animals. His real reason for dropping biology, he told me, was his difficulty in writing. After abandoning this course, Emile attempted to incorporate his love of animals into his art pieces. For instance, his love of reptiles led him to mold a reptile in clay onto his coursework sculpture. Socially, he also found a part-time post in a local reptile shop where he had earlier conducted work experience. In his interview, he told me that he enjoyed working with, and being around, these animals. Emile also told me that he planned to continue this fascination and apply for a course in the study and care of reptiles when he left school.

Emile's Projects

During the course of the study, Emile was observed, then interviewed at intervals and also recorded a diary for two A-level projects involving the making of clay pieces, such as jars and pots. These first pieces of coursework were followed by two larger projects that formed a major proportion of his final A-level grade. I again observed these and also recorded their processes through photographs (Hayhoe, 2005). The assessment for these projects was not only based on the final piece, but also included his workings (photographs, drawings, etc.) and eventually a written description. What now follows is a description of the observed projects.

The first of Emile's projects was the clay sculpture of a cliff face with small water reservoirs and a lizard climbing its rough face that, he explained, was initially inspired by a study carried out mainly through reptile magazines. Emile began by making maquettes of the sculpture in clay and simple technical drawings of the sculpture-making process. These were to include notes on measurements and technical aspects. Again, writing seemed to be a problem, and he appeared to do these only after a great deal of reluctance and after a long period of time—and only on the insistence of Gerard. As he explained in an excerpt from one edition of his notes, "What I find most difficult about my...education at A level is having to write things down and keep a log of what I am doing. And also to stick with one idea" (Emile, personal communication, March 2000).

After planning his work, Emile made the final cliff face in three discrete pieces, each made of large clay slabs. The middle section of his sculpture had a small reservoir with a hole in the bottom, which represented a lake. Inside the sculpture there was to be a further reservoir in the large bottom section, and there was also supposed to be a small electrical pump that would carry water up through the middle. Emile said that he wanted the water to emerge from the top section, trickle down the front, and out into the outer reservoir. However, by the end of the project this element remained unfinished.

The timing of this project relied on self-motivation, as it was carried out individually during lesson times and Emile's individual study time. He was supposed to have minimal supervision or instruction during his projects, although he had been taught many of his skills previously and preferred relatively little didactic teaching, appearing to rely on experimentation instead. However, despite not having a large hands-on teaching role, Gerard provided a great deal of practical supervision. For instance, he helped to lift the clay and provided advice on its quality. He also helped with basic chores, such as arranging instruments and tools.

During the project, I also noted that Gerard played a major role in making a lizard to be placed on the face of the cliff. This was first developed by photographing a real lizard from Emile's shop, molding a copy of this image in clay, and then adhering it to the outside of the cliff face when it was still wet. After this initial attempt, however, Emile did not appear to be pleased with his lizard model, and Gerard felt that it was not up to A-level standard. Consequently, Gerard suggested that they buy a toy model of a lizard and mold a clay model from its impression. The result was a great deal more successful, but suggested that Gerard was always around as a form of safety net for Emile.

The brief for Emile's second project was that it was to be an individual study of a form of art he had not previously encountered, for which Emile chose Racu pottery. Racu is an ancient form of pottery originating from Japan, which dates back over thousands of years. In the examination board's description of the project's assessment, schools were told that the students were allowed less supervision than previously afforded them, and were expected to contribute more written work than before.

During my observation of this project, I found that Emile appeared to do noticeably less work on this project than he did on the first. This attitude appeared to be counter to his initial plans, which I recorded during his initial interview. For instance, I noted that in his interview and diary reports Emile planned to dig his own clay from the school grounds, as he had done for a similar project, as it would provide more authentic material. He had also said that he was to build a Racu kiln just outside of the class, near a nature area he had worked on for an earlier biology project. But none of these seemingly elaborate plans came to fruition. He did make some Racu pots on the classroom wheel from clay ordered through a supplier and beat the outsides in the traditional style; he also conducted Internet research and made contact with a local Racu potter who was to help him research this technique. However, I discovered in the course of my visits that he neither stayed in contact with the potter nor conducted the required amount of further research, and his hands-on work on the artwork during lesson times became less and less.

Emile appeared to reserve the remainder of his time for this project during individual study periods and evenings where, theoretically, he could be monitored less. And although Gerard again appeared to provide practical help with this project by, for instance, showing Emile how to use the modeling wheel and demonstrating the Racu beating technique, in accordance with the examination board's wishes, he provided no direct teaching.

Emile's Behaviour: Avoidance and Denial
The attitudes shown by Emile's teachers in his early mainstream classes showed the negative effects of their lack of training and

resource provision. Even though they had to include students with disabilities in their classes, they either had not been provided with a weight of evidence that students with disabilities could undertake tasks as other students in their classes could, or they were not interested in helping them because they did not know how or were afraid to try. This provision can be seen in contrast to the training that teachers in schools for the blind received and the experiences they had. In my observations, it appeared that this led them to believe their students were more capable of undertaking art tasks, and had a framework with which to include them in their lessons.

In terms of his behaviour, it would seem that Emile's case highlights issues not observed in the adult case studies featured in the previous chapter. Emile's extremely negative early experiences of freehand drawing and literacy had led him to display what was negative learning behaviour, avoiding the learning outcomes that he knew existed.

Emile was particularly reluctant to take risks in academic tasks that involved freehand drawing or literacy, and in many ways—despite his experience—Emile reacted as an inexperienced student would. He approached ambiguous tasks and assessment criteria, which could have been interpreted in a variety of ways by the examiners, by showing little self-confidence and actively avoiding tasks he had negative experiences of as a child. For instance, he explained that his unwillingness to continue with his Racu pottery was due to his reluctance to conduct the research and writing required for the project.

> Emile also tells me that he has not worked [any] further on his Racu project because he is reluctant to write things down. On this point, I asked him why he is reluctant and he replies, "because I'm no good at it—grammar, spelling,

everything." As a result Emile also says that, "I have a real rush to get things done now..." (S. Hayhoe, observation notes, February 2001)

At the same time, I observed him noticeably enjoying and behaving with confidence in tasks he had only learnt since going to New College, such as sculpting with clay. In these circumstances, I conjectured that he pursued these new tasks because they provided him with the self-esteem and confidence that the others denied him, leaving him to concentrate on them at the expense of others even though he knew that this would work against his assessment criteria.

For instance, Emile displayed negative learning behaviour and what seemed a lack of self-confidence by not reading or researching for his Racu project, and by only drawing simple, often purposely rough and ambiguous engineering-style drawings for his sculpture project. This behaviour was in marked contrast to his confident approach to the creation of pottery, of which he had no experience at his early mainstream school.

Most notably, because Emile was aware of what was expected of his coursework but chose to sacrifice his future for his elaborate experiments with clay, he concentrated much less on the drawing elements of his coursework, which would have been lucrative in terms of his marks. As a result, it seems possible that Emile's behaviour showed that he was rejecting the logic that he could achieve a high mark at A level, and instead applied a different logic that developing a lack of worth would fulfil a different social and cultural purpose. Consequently, even when Gerard disciplined Emile and made him draw, he merely presented basic lines and the dimensions and measurements of his sculpture. He did not attempt three-dimensional visualisations as he was supposed to, and in my notes I recorded what seemed to me to be low opinions of his own graphic ability. One of these excerpts is given here:

> Finally, I asked Emile whether he had done any more drawing this month [and he] replied no free hand drawing. However, he had done some more engineering drawings to show how water will flow from the reservoir within the sculpture and out over the moulded front surface of the piece. I then asked whether he regarded this as an example of an engineering drawing, to which he replies that, it is an [Emile] drawing. It won't resemble anything. (S. Hayhoe, observation notes, February 2001)

It is possible that Emile simply did not like drawing for personal or aesthetic reasons; however, given his extreme reaction to such tasks and knowing how this would affect his marks, this seemed unlikely. Furthermore, even though he told me that he became frustrated with certain mechanical elements of his sculptural construction and did not enjoy doing them, he continued with them, seeming to know they would present a nicer piece and a higher final grade.

A further possibility I considered was that Emile's experiences of personal educational success in clay work after attending New College had become *habit forming* as a means of self-expression, particularly as they had greater tactile qualities and were easily acceptable forms of communication. He could hence enjoy this form of art not just as an expressive outlet but also as an instance of academic achievement, which would then have become a self-fulfilling cycle of increased self-esteem in this field as he concentrated on this form of educational task at the expense of others in subsequent educational projects. These increased his sense of self-confidence as he continued.

Examples of Emile's behaviour tended to suggest that my latter conjecture was a better explanation of his behaviour. For instance,

I found that Emile substituted drawing for clay work in early exercises at New College. During these tasks, he particularly adapted figurative representations, which he said he found very difficult, into exercises involving the abstract moulding of clay, such as his series of clay masks. During the same year at New College, Emile found that Gerard set projects that assessed him on his use of freehand drawing skills that, he told me during one interview, he renegotiated to favour his new clay moulding techniques.

This process allowed Emile to adapt his preferred clay relief[3] form of three-dimensional representations as a substitute for his drawings in his art classes. Although he had not experienced clay moulding using this method or form before entering New College, he appeared to hold fewer negative expectations about it, and this suited his aim of finding a form of art that allowed him to avoid drawing. This is illustrated in the extract from my notes at the time:

> Emile then tells me that after these initial attempts at mask making, he had made a further mask based on an African tribal sculpture...He tells me that he can not copy very well [whether two- or three-dimensionally]. For this reason, the form [of the following models] were decided during their making process (that is he made up the form of the African model from imagination, rather than attempting a facsimile). Emile says that he has also used the same technique for the same reasons whilst creating his clay pots. As an example, Emile explains that when he was first making several clay pots they were supposed to be of a fairly conventional design. However as he began throwing them, he felt that they formed themselves into an unorthodox shape. (S. Hayhoe, observation notes, April 2001)

Emile's behaviour, therefore, was at least in part motivated more by the negative aspects of avoiding embarrassment and decreasing his worth than what seemed to be more positive social and cultural motivations, such as the need to expand his knowledge as best he could, or even pure creative or emotional expressions of ideas. In this way, his behaviour contrasted in a very stark manner to that of another student in the group. And this brings me to the case study of this student, whom I called Anna, to which this chapter now turns.

ANNA, THE GIRL WHO SAW IN THE DARK

Anna's Educational Background

Anna was registered as legally blind, the result of being born with a condition called cone dystrophy—a restricted number of cone cells in her retinas distorted her visual acuity radically and caused photophobia and eye stigmas. As a result, she found it difficult to focus on images and had complete colour blindness; a fuller medical description of a condition with similar symptoms can be found in the British neurologist Oliver Sack's (1996) book, *The Island of the Colour Blind*. As she told me in her interview about her blindness,

> I'd say I have 75% of the detail that I need. Twenty-five percent, however, is missing. I cannot see facial expressions from more than 6 metres away. I also...cannot focus very well. And because of this my eyes wobble around, and try and make up for that movement, until they are actually in focus again. (Anna, personal communication, March 2000)

Anna was 16 at the beginning of this study. She had been to mainstream schools when she was younger, where the learning experiences, she felt, had been generally positive. In her interview, Anna told me that she only moved to New College when her sight deteriorated substantially and her mainstream school could no longer support her. At this point, her local authority supported sending her and other similarly physically disabled students to special schools. I was later told in an interview with the principal of New College that this was unusual for education authorities in the United Kingdom.

In terms of her early experiences of early mainstream classes, Anna said that she was encouraged to do all of the art tasks her peers were given and also was provided help in undertaking them. Although she had initially faced difficulties at mainstream school because of her sight problems and had particular problems using colour in her work because of her total colour blindness, after a long period of practice, when reaching the latter stages of her compulsory education, she had little problem fitting in with all aspects of her art lessons.

For example, in one instance she explained that her mother helped her to design a system of labeling her pens and pencils during her drawing lessons to enable her to relate objects to colours. She persevered with the problem, and eventually adjusted to making some sense of their composition by finding verbal metaphors for these colours. The following is one of these explanations of her colour work that she recorded:

> I always found art difficult in mainstream because of my colour vision, or lack of. You know I was always having to ask people what colour things were, like paints. With my pens and pencils, however, I usually labelled them up and then took them into school, so I knew what colour was what. When it came to mixing paints and things I had real trouble. And I've never been very good at using paints, because I can't even see when paints have run into each other on the actual painting. And sometimes they can turn out a real mess. So, yeah, I found that difficult.

> That got easier though towards GCSE. I was more independent, I could more, tell more easily, you know, what colours that I was using. Probably because I got used to recognising them, because they are shades of grey as I see them. (Anna, personal communication, March 2000)

In her interview, Anna also explained that, after transferring schools to New College and studying art and graphic design in its upper school, she had overcome many of the remaining problems of representing colour that her previous system had not addressed. As a result, having confronted this issue earlier on, she found that during her initial A-level ceramics exercises she could find striking analogies of colour with tone, which helped her recognise glazes in particular. In her descriptions of her personal learning history, Anna also said that she had been drawing throughout her school career and had drawn or painted at home for as long as she could remember.

In her nonart subjects, she also felt that she was treated relatively normally at her first school, and so she came to choose art at A level for more objective reasons. She said that she was taking A-level art as she enjoyed this form of creative activity and was successful in both of her similar, previous GCSE courses. Later in this study, Anna also told me that she had been accepted for an art foundation course at university—which is a year-long course for those wanting to take a degree in art. I also discovered that she was heavily involved in theatrical activities and continued with two other A levels during this research, achieving excellence in these areas as well.

> My art education? Well from a very early age, I've loved drawing. I loved drawing in primary school and secondary school. I did art GCSE for which I got an A. And I've always enjoyed doing art outside of school as well. I am

a very imaginative person, and I find that I can express myself quite easily with art. I've still got some of my pieces from when I was younger, and looking at them now they seem quite funny, but at the time they were very good. Yeah, I love art very much. (Anna, personal communication, March 2000)

Anna's Projects
At the beginning of the observations, Anna was just finishing a life drawing and a ceramic tile exercise. Although these pieces did not contribute to her A-level assessment, the photographs of her pieces are shown in the illustrations. Her ceramic tiles were colourfully glazed designs featuring dolphins leaping out of the water, and the life drawings were a series of outlines of a naked woman, which were also presented in different colours. She presented this later piece on black sugar paper, which she told me would highlight its colours. These were soon followed by two main assessed exercises.

After completing her short exercises, Anna began individual, A-level coursework projects, the first of which was based on an interpretation of a sculpture by Canova, entitled *Cupid and Psyche*. The original of this piece featured the god and goddess staring into each other's eyes and was sculpted in marble. Although Anna had not seen the original firsthand, she told me that she had taken a photocopy of its illustration from a textbook she found in the school's library, and that she was particularly struck by it as soon as she saw it because it had such an enchanting theme.

Anna began this project by sketching figures in the same position as the sculpture, and then developed further drawings, which abstracted the two bodies into a single flowing shape. Anna then chose her materials for the sculpture through a process of experimentation with various media and coverings, chosen for their practical as well as their aesthetic qualities. She eventually chose to try the first attempts at this sculpture in clay. An excerpt of this process is given next:

> So I made a few maquettes. I then tried drawing those. I drew them on, like, brown envelope material paper. I used charcoal, black crayon and white paint to create a black and white abstract image of the abstract maquettes. I then moved on and, using other famous sculptures that I'd found in books, I drew them in the same fashion with the charcoal and white paint. I drew them and made them abstract as well. And I intend to make those into maquettes as well. The other day, I found a sculpture with four people, it's a family group. It almost seems like they're all holding hands, but they're intertwined, and it's like abstract rounded shapes, and that got me onto thinking that, well, instead of just putting one person into a sculpture then you can put more than one. And I'm starting, I'm exploring that idea now. I've looked at a sculpture called *The Rape of the [Sabine]*, which has got three people in it. It is very emotional, and it's a very emotional sculpture. And there's an awful lot of movement in it. And I've drawn that as a line drawing, abstract. And I hope to make that into a maquette, also design some more of my own. And then finally, I'm going to make one or two large pieces, which will be my final piece for that project. And then I'll move on again. (Anna, personal communication, March 2000)

Initially, Anna made the small maquette of the sculpture to see if her design was practically feasible, as she had to be certain that the wings were not too heavy. After successfully creating this small piece, she continued to make the full-size sculpture in the same way. Unfortunately, this sculpture proved impractical, as its wings were too heavy and fell off, and so Anna changed the material to mud rock on newspaper, which was lighter and more flexible.

After further experimentation, however, Anna told me that she found the mud rock was suitable for the bodies but not the wings of the sculpture. This discovery was followed by further unsuccessful experiments with real feather wings, after which Anna said that she felt it was more prudent to make the wings from stiff card, which she also found a use for as halos over their heads. After making these objects, she decorated them with gold paint and patterns of broken CDs.

In the course of this project, Anna found that she could be increasingly creative and take risks. Consequently, as she made the main bodies of the sculpture, she told me that she noticed they resembled tree trunks, and she liked this similarity. As a consequence, Anna decided to abstract the figures into a single form, similar to the original drawings she had made, forming the arms into branches between the two bodies. This whole form was then sprayed with a golden-brown paint and the faces of the sculpture were developed as more straightforward profile drawings.

Anna's second project was her individual study. After a great deal of discussion, this turned out to be a black and white photography project focusing on the subject of people's body parts—an exercise she had begun during her holidays. At first she chose this subject as she became fascinated with photographing people's hands, but then she found that these photographs often appeared to compare people's wrinkled skin to tree bark—she remarked on this in particular on more than one occasion.

After these initial experiments, Anna said that she persuaded her friend and then her mother to have their hands photographed—she was particularly pleased with the photographs of her mother's hands, as they were older and more wrinkled. When I asked why she liked this texture more than others she had worked with, she answered that it was their tonal qualities. This topic, she said, permeated other work on this subject too. The plan of this project is elaborated in this excerpt from my notes:

> During her Christmas holiday, Anna plans to take more black and white pictures. She says, "I really, really enjoy it." She also says that she would spend three hours after school in the dark room in New College if she had to, as the project is that important to her. Anna also said that it gives her real senses of achievement when she gets an image right the way she wants it.
>
> Anna shows me a series of black and white photographs that she took during her previous half-term holiday. This series is of what she considers to be interesting faces of people she either knows or found in London. She says that she particularly enjoys [her] images of old men with teeth missing. (S. Hayhoe, observation notes, November 2000)

Anna learnt how to develop her own work using the school's darkrooms during this project, and she enlisted outside help from a local professional photographer to give her advice about the processes involved. This professional also took Anna out to learn about landscape photography, which culminated in a portfolio of written descriptions and research of process and photographs that was submitted to the examination board and, as I soon afterwards discovered, was later exhibited at the college for a short period in recognition of its high quality.

During this project, Anna appeared to receive little didactic instruction from Gerard, and during lesson periods, he only appeared to intervene with the practical engineering elements of the sculpture's construction. Consequently, Anna worked through many of her own creative problems and learnt through self-experimentation, an intention in common with the syllabus and its assessment criteria. Indeed, in my observations I only recorded two instances of Anna receiving practical help: the first was when she asked Gerard to help her physically stick the wings to her sculpture, and the second was a discussion with him to inform her choice of mudrock as a medium of construction for the body of her sculpture.

Anna's Behaviour: Experimentation and Risk
In terms of this book's examination of social and cultural influences on attitudes, Anna's early mainstream teachers had not been overly affected by negative social or cultural expectations, nor by their lack of training. The expectations Anna had been given were high, as her teachers included her in the same assessed exercises as the rest of her classmates in their environment. A possible explanation of this phenomenon is that her early school teachers, despite their lack of training, Anna told me they had previous experience of teaching a student with a visual impairment. Furthermore, she also had access to lesson equipment for students with visual impairments. Thus, her school seemed to have been prepared for her entry.

It is possible that Anna was simply extremely gifted at art, and that this was demonstrated in her classes. However, I felt that this would not necessarily give her confidence, as many others without talent have had unfounded confidence, and those with it seemed unconfident. This would suggest that confidence is not necessarily a product of talent.

Therefore, it seemed that a more probable explanation was that Anna's school had managed to adapt teaching strategies and realistic expectations of blind and visually impaired students before Anna attended, and their approach instilled her with confidence. Hence, in terms of their development of a strand of expectation, it was important for Anna that, despite their lack of training in this field, her mainstream teachers and her parents had developed a more normal outlook for her as a capable student, rather than one with a visual impairment. It was this personal history that, I felt, had affected her later classroom behaviour, as she had similar expectations to people with normal sight, therefore providing her with high visual cultural expectations.

Anna's confidence was evident in her early observations, when she behaved as an experienced student in mainstream education would. In these, she took risks in an attempt to find the most workable and attractive piece in each project, and she showed that she had a genuine love of drawing despite her earlier difficulties. This attitude resulted in no notable instances of avoiding any of her tasks, even during lessons that, she told me, she found difficult.

For instance, Anna said in her early discussions that she felt she was capable of taking part in tasks with a two-dimensional visual and colour element. Consequently, she took further risks with bright colour in her drawing tasks, and even when she said she found them hard, she was never discouraged. This, it could be argued, was vital to her artistic development as it allowed her to negotiate different techniques with her teachers' assessment schemes, and ameliorated many of the negative physical problems caused by her blindness.

In addition, Anna was willing to risk sketching out her ideas as both representational and abstract drawings in her final coursework, even though she must have realised that it would risk being judged severely as a consequence. Similarly, she had no fear of taking further risks with colour in her sculptural work as well, and she did not avoid her tasks related to this aspect of her work, even though the potential for this avoidance existed because of her colour blindness—her brief stated that her sculpture did not need to contain colour, but she chose to ignore it. The following excerpt is an example she gave of these experiments in her notes:

> My maquettes came out of the kiln today, the maquettes of the girl sitting down. And I've started to glaze those. I'm glazing them because there are three of them. One of them is tall and exaggerated. One of them is like slunk, and looks like its melting. And the other is more of a realistic shape. I decided to glaze them, well paint two of them and glaze one of them. I'm glazing the taller one a sort of reddy brown. And I've used stone paints on the other two, one of which is like a limestone or granite, and the other is like sand, slightly sparkly, sort of greyey, orangey, yellowey colour, which I like. I think they look very good so far. Because they are not man made shapes, they are natural looking shapes, you know, very smooth looking shapes. And I thought the natural looking colour would look best. However, I did try glaze, as I said, on the tall figure, just to see. I mean the glaze might look better once it is fired up. It's just an experiment. (Anna, personal communication, March 2000)

During these tasks, I also noted that Anna again experimented with further high-risk techniques, which eventually provided her with a different understanding of colour. In addition, she explained that she found her approach to clay work in her mainstream school and New College had largely negated her disability. Although she admitted that she encountered problems because of her blindness, this did not damage her belief that she could succeed. Furthermore, her success in this and similar tasks, as well as her willingness to take risks, appeared to make her even too ambitious at times, which led in turn to its own problems, as such unnecessary risk taking for the sake of pushing the envelope threatened her academic success and her eventual grade.

Examples of this behaviour appeared in many instances in Anna's notes. For instance, Gerard told me in his interview that her willingness to try too much led her to experiment with objects that could not be assessed as part of her coursework. In addition, when she described the complex process of producing the wings of her sculpture—even though she had to change techniques twice—she took further risks by making the wings with different materials. She used real feathers at first, and then, when these proved impractical, she experimented with card and spray paint. These, she said, provided a stunning result, although she also felt that it was a great deal of work to achieve what was in effect a frivolity.

Finally, I felt Anna's success in her art classes, and her positive experiences of the visual arts provided her with the confidence to try new experiences and take higher risks with new topics, even during her assessed projects, and suggested that her self-esteem could be transferred to new forms of artistic techniques and methods. Thus, in Anna's experience of art, risk taking appeared to be a valid learning technique on which to build classroom exercises.

For instance, despite never having tried photography before her A-level coursework, Anna was very willing to risk experimenting with taking and developing photographs, and enlisted the help of a local photographer without fear of risking her self-esteem or confidence. During this project, she had learnt how to develop film and had gone on visits with the photographer to search for sites, with relative freedom and without fear of failure. Even though these tasks involved a discourse with an expert that would highlight errors in her project, again she seemed unafraid of taking such risks.

What now follows is a conclusion of the findings from both of these case studies.

ATTITUDES AND THEIR CONSEQUENCES

These case studies suggest that a complex picture of experiences existed in Emile's and Anna's mainstream schooling, which had implications throughout their later education. Emile was psychologically excluded from many art tasks that his fellow sighted students had the chance to try, even though he was physically included in their classes. This might have been a result of the lack of training on the part of his teachers, which remained unconsidered by their schools, although it is also possible that their style of education was fundamentally different from the style needed by such a specialist case.

In addition, a similar reason could be suggested for Emile's lack of resources in this school that left him lacking many fundamental educational skills. Anna, on the other hand, had positive experiences of art during her mainstream schooling. Although it appeared that her teachers had also not received formal training, her school had educated a student who was visually impaired before and so had a greater understanding of Anna's potential and her practical needs. As a result, and with the support of her family, Anna negotiated and developed methods of overcoming her disability, and therefore negated her lack of vision.

I have to admit that I cannot claim the amount of evidence presented in this part of the study showed significant patterns of behaviour. However, it does support a notion that the effects of exclusion have not been truly considered in different subjects in terms of its effects on behaviour. The fact that there was such a marked difference in behaviour between Emile and Anna, despite their same quantities of experience, shows that this factor in isolation can at least in part explain an avoidance of what are highly positive risks.

For instance, even though Emile had taken art when he first attended New College, he avoided tasks that he had bad experiences of when he was younger and attempted to make their frame of reference more ambiguous. At New College, however, he attempted tasks he had no experience of, although they were ambiguous—that is, he had no definite subject or brief—and he could have failed easily.

For example, Emile avoided drawing even though he had experience of studying this subject, suggesting that he had a low self-worth in his ability in this aspect of the visual arts. In addition, when he was presented with the new task of moulding clay masks to form two-dimensional reliefs, he approached it without fear. He also attempted to make the subjects of these exercises more ambiguous, and therefore risky, by making shapes that referred to abstract subjects, as it allowed him freedom from reproduction exercises that were part of his previous drawing exercises.

Furthermore, Emile's drive to find a subject he could excel in led to a further motivation to attempt tasks that bore no relation to those he had previously had negative experiences of. For instance, as soon as Emile had positive experiences of clay work, he emphasised this element of his artwork at the expense of drawing and researching, which involved high levels of literacy, even though he knew that in assessed exercises this would lead to a reduction of his grade. This also led Emile to choose art as a form of media in which he could pursue his passion for reptiles, rather than studying biology, which required high levels of literacy.

Conversely, because Anna was presented with normal expectations in her early, mainstream art classes, she behaved in a way that was similar to a mainstream student, which led her to negate what were potentially many disabling factors in her education. For instance, although Anna had no colour perception, she worked and experimented with colour confidently during her observations, and she had a high sense of self-esteem and confidence in these tasks.

This ability to work with colour seemed to be at least partly because her family and teachers found methods of analogising colour, allowing her to develop a notion of what colour could represent in art. This, she said, also made the task of colouring a less difficult and confusing one. For example, she knew that the label green represented grass and the label blue represented sky, until she had developed enough knowledge of its use to experiment on her own.

Finally, it also appears that experimentation became a trait she generated from within herself, from a sense of self-worth in her ability to create successful artworks, even when her assessments demanded a more cautious approach. Thus, Anna developed so much self-esteem that she was willing to go beyond the task she had been set in order to develop what she felt were alternative educational goals, even though this feasibly reduced her future acceptance by an art college. For instance, during the observations, Anna took a great deal of time experimenting with different materials and media in order to perfect her wings.

This appeared to worry her teacher, Gerard, because he was concerned that she was not concentrating on other aspects of the sculpture's design, even though she was wholly capable of attaining a high grade. As a result, when she reached a certain point in her experimentation that risked overstepping the lines of what he felt was sensibly achievable, Gerard steered Anna back onto her main task and away from what she felt were her real goals.

These issues themselves raised further questions that I felt needed to be addressed during the study. As I only studied two students at New College, I wondered whether Emile's and Anna's experiences and behaviours were comparable to those of other students in similar institutions and under different circumstances and contexts—that is, were they related to general modes of behaviour or just those of this isolated social group? Was this a local problem? Was this issue only a contemporary problem? Moreover, was it restricted to English education in schools for the blind?

In order to address these questions, I arranged interviews with teachers in other schools for the blind in England and the United States. This gave a good, English-speaking cultural comparison, as North America had gone through a similar process of integration of blind students. I also interviewed Gerard from New College as a part of this study. It is the findings of these interviews that I now address in the following chapter.

Endnotes

1. Each county or borough in the United Kingdom is responsible for administering its schools and students. The body based in each council is called a Local Education Authority.
2. Photographs of Emile's and Anna's work are given in the illustrations section of this book.
3. This is a quasi two-dimensional reproduction technique using partially raised surfaces.

CHAPTER 6

ART TEACHERS OF THE BLIND: UNDERSTANDING THE ROLE OF EXPERIENCES

INTRODUCTION

This chapter describes the experiences and observations of teachers in schools for the blind in the United Kingdom and the United States in different learning environments and cultures in order to discover whether any behavioural threads existed outside of those I observed at New College. Before going any further, however, I should emphasise that my description was never designed to be a cross-cultural study (i.e., a study of the differences or similarities between cultures). Rather, it was designed to examine whether the same behaviour was observable despite different educational systems, societies, and social groups. The responses I found in common, therefore, were more likely to be seen as general human responses.

The reason I concentrated the non-English part of the study in the United States was merely practicality. The initial parts of this study were conducted with the cooperation of the charity Art Beyond Sight, which is based in New York City. This focused on a series of visits to museums, galleries, and schools for the blind in three U.S. states, where I observed issues such as access and teaching, and where I managed to conduct a series of interviews with the teachers based in their art departments. An initial review of these observations and interviews hinted that the United States had undergone strikingly similar experiences to the United Kingdom since integrating blind students into art exhibitions and lessons.

In addition, it appeared from this research that, similar to mainstream school teachers in England, mainstream U.S. teachers were not provided with extra training and appeared to have limited resourcing to facilitate the inclusion of students who were blind or visually impaired. Whilst visiting these schools in the United States, I found that there was also a sharing of educational theory and practice between the United States and England—including study visits from academics at Birmingham University, my own university at the time, which had strong academic links with New College, Worcester. Consequently, students and teachers found themselves in similar educational circumstances in terms of art education.

The description of this part of the study that now follows in this chapter is split into the following three parts: a description of the teachers and the educational cultures that they worked in, the experiences and observations described in the interviews with the art teachers, and, finally, the conclusions I drew from these interviews. These now follow with a description of the education systems and cultural differences of the United Kingdom and the United States.

THE TEACHERS AND THEIR EDUCATIONAL BACKGROUNDS

The Development of U.S. and English Educational Systems

Before beginning my description of these teachers' experiences, it is important to clarify the differences and similarities between English and U.S. school education for the blind in order to appreciate and understand the teacher's narratives in these pages. I begin this process with an explanation of the two national approaches to education and policy making.

Although culturally different in their modern contexts, England and the United States have a great deal in common in terms of their educational roots and the history or their broader blind culture. Consequently, even though the two countries have evolved many miles apart in the 250 years since U.S. independence, their contemporary histories still often have similar political movements and social trends. Primarily, these ties continue not only through our common language, but also through our governments, religious ethics, and also a largely common social ancestry. In this context, the most interesting of these was, of course, the integration of disabled students in a mainstream curriculum.

There are, however, distinct political and educational differences that result from our contemporary histories that should also be taken into account in the context of this study. Firstly, U.S. education is not centrally controlled by a national government as it is in England. Therefore, U.S. educators do not have a national curriculum as England does, and their syllabi are more dispersed and at the command of the individual teacher and the school. The official policy of integrating children with disabilities has been in place relatively longer in a number of U.S. states than in England. Many U.S. states began legal integration during the 1970s, whereas in England as a whole it began in 1981, although both countries had been unofficially integrating children with disabilities before this era.

In both countries, assessment also has different connotations. In the United States, it is only necessary to attain credit in an arts subject. To attain credit, a student has to demonstrate they have reached a subjective target, often negotiated with their teachers, and this is assessed locally. In England, children must attain nationally recognised targets of competence throughout their school careers, and schools' and students' performances compete nationally and locally in league tables, which are often published by the government and mass media. And thus, in terms of assessment of their social worth, English schools will be brought to account far more often than their U.S. counterparts, and English students with physical disabilities at least are expected to perform similarly well to their mainstream counterparts in all of their academic subjects.

What now follows is an outline of the teachers and the schools involved in the study. The names of teachers and institutions, with the exception of New College, are kept anonymous.

The Teachers and Their Schools
Interviews were conducted with four U.S. art teachers in different schools for the blind, one U.S. peripatetic teacher who supported blind students in art classes, and four English art teachers in schools for the blind. The U.S. teachers and their schools were given these pseudonyms: Taylor from Ashton Gate, Cassie from Highbury, Stacy from Highfield Road, Petra from St. Andrew's, and Cheryl from The Walker's Stadium. The English teachers

and their schools were given these pseudonyms: Steve from Anfield, Harry from The Valley, Asia from The Hawthorns, and Gerard from New College (I decided to keep his name as it was in the previous chapter).

All of these teachers had been practicing for more than 15 years and had taught in mainstream schools before their current posts. Five of these teachers had also previously been professional artists. Three were men and six were women—this gender split seemed to be fairly typical for art teachers in schools for the blind, although this was not a precise science, as there are never enough art teachers in schools for the blind to be able to conduct a meaningful survey.

Notably, none of the teachers I interviewed were blind or visually impaired themselves, and none of the schools that I approached had ever employed a blind or visually impaired art teacher. All of the teachers involved in the study had been trained to teach students who were blind at universities in their own countries. In the United States, this training either consisted of a supplementary course to their degree or a post-graduate certificate course whilst they were teaching, whilst in England the teachers took an extra qualification after completing their first degree and initial teacher training, which either consisted of a first degree and a postgraduate certificate or diploma in education, or taking an extended teaching degree which was equivalent. In England, the specialist qualification for the instruction of pupils in classes where the majority of pupils were blind was a legal requirement, and was usually taken after teachers had begun their first posts.

Apart from The Valley, which was founded by its county council, all of the schools featured in the study were originally formed as asylums or charity-run schools for the blind. The majority of these schools, however, had been subsumed by Local

Educational Authorities (LEAs) in England, or state or county authorities in the United States. Only a few remained as independent charities or were run by larger charities. The students in these schools mainly came from wide geographic areas and, apart from The Hawthorns, were accepted boarding students. The schools also had relatively small student bodies: Around 200 was the maximum number, and class sizes were very small. I observed a maximum of four students in any of the classes I visited, and children up to 16 years old also tended to have classroom assistants to help in lessons—although after this age examination classes tended to have no assistants.

What now follows is a description of the teachers' methods, philosophies, and styles that I observed during this study.

The Teachers' Practice

All of the teachers I visited in schools for the blind appeared to present positive expectations of their students' work, and several of the teachers described creating a tactile language as the basis of their teaching. Some teachers also described the need to connect with blind children through topics of particular interest to them, as they had such different experiences from mainstream society. For instance, Harry from The Valley described his approach to teaching children who were registered blind by highlighting the importance of building tactile symbols from as early an age as possible. He also said that he liaised with the teachers in his junior school and used these symbols there, in order to provide a sense of continuity in their art education.

Furthermore, many of the schools that participated in the study had students with other physical and learning disabilities, which appeared to me to be common with the conditions that caused their blindness, such as those who had suffered brain tumours or had Down's syndrome. These children, it was thought, presented many difficulties in the way that they interacted socially and educationally with the rest of their classes. These teachers felt that many also had difficulties when trying to concentrate or when they were without attention for any length of time. All of these factors aside, almost all of the teachers also felt that as long as their students had no previous negative experiences of art, they always attempted their tasks, whether or not they went on to chose art as an elected subject.

In one of his interviews with me, Gerard from New College also described engaging students through a combination of tactile and verbal discussions during lessons. For example, when he began teaching his students, he told me that he discussed subjects they were interested in and then allowed them to explore these subjects through the design of artefacts in several different media. He then explained he would take a problem-solving approach to setting many of their art tasks, often giving his students the freedom to experiment and find techniques that suited their particular needs—whether they related to their blindness or to other learning difficulties. What follows is the short excerpt from one such discussion in which he describes this technique:

> I just looked at things that they might be interested in. Themes that they might be interested in. Things common to them. Not things that were totally alien to them; so that they were at least working on something that they might have an interest in; even if they weren't particularly interested in art. You know, I have kids that are fairly bright and set them problem-solving exercises, practical problem-solving exercises.
>
> You know, they were useful to do, because again there didn't necessarily have to be an artistic outcome. They were also getting a process, so you know this had taken up a long period of time and wasn't always being successful, but I think I put things like involvement and interest and enjoyment at the top of the list of what I want to achieve from the lesson.

Obviously there are...hopefully learning outcomes and they will differ from pupil to pupil, but unless you can engage them in an activity then you basically aren't going to get anywhere. So I was looking for that involvement, and I tried to tap in to what ever they were interested in. (Gerard, personal communication, February 2000)

What now follows in this chapter is a description of the teachers' observations during their years of practice.

EXPERIENCES OF TEACHING ART IN ENGLAND AND THE UNITED STATES

In these interviews, I found that many of the teachers from both countries recognised that students who had been educated in mainstream classes before schools for the blind, or those who had been educated in schools before legal integration began, had experienced exclusion and segregation in many of their art lessons. Moreover, many of these students, if this exclusion was suffered at a relatively young age, were more likely to avoid similar tasks in their upper schools or adult classes, even when they were surrounded by peers with similar disabilities.

For instance, the English teacher, Asia, found that adults taught before legal integration were reluctant to approach art tasks when she provided outreach courses many years later. In her judgment, this same lack of confidence applied to students of all ages, abilities, and disabilities who had negative or no experiences of art before entering their courses. In addition, she explained that these social attitudes of mainstream art teachers affected these students more than the physical or mental ability of their students.

These English experiences were comparable to those described by Petra in the United States. Like Asia, she found that when students who were blind or visually impaired had been excluded from mainstream art classes, they would more often than not acquire evidence to support these negative beliefs about their own ability, which in turn often led to an avoidance of tasks in art lessons. What follows is part of Petra's description of this observation:

> There's a place, I don't know exactly where...It's probably different for each person. There's a kind of inner reception or place, where you're willing to be an artist; even though you might have had very little experience with artistic materials. And then there's a time when a student will just say "not for me, this is not something that I'm ever going to enjoy, I'd rather take music, or I'd rather do gardening or something".
>
> Because they don't feel that they can express themselves in what we call the fine artistic genre of thinking, they just don't want to go there. Mostly, and with very few exceptions, [these are] students who come here after finishing somewhere else [in mainstream education]. Some come here after their teens to take a year at [St. Andrew's] to fill in the gap on technology, mobility, and occasionally they'll have an art class...
>
> They would have been [mainstream] all the way through. Most of the students I have had come in after that time from regular secondary schools, I've only had one who had interest in art...They're ready to do something else. They're ready to get their act together to be a college student, or they want to go into some kind of vocational training...But as far as art goes, most of the time they don't feel they have time for it. (Petra, personal communication, February 2004)

Furthermore, Harry and Taylor from England and the United States, respectively, both provided similar descriptions of students who had poor experiences as a result of negative expectations in their early mainstream schools. Both said that these students' expectations were instilled through their early art teachers, who were often informed by social attitudes to blindness rather than by a broad experience of teaching students who were blind. Consequently, these students had developed an ability to avoid tasks during art classes in their schools for the blind later in their academic careers.

In one instance, Harry described teaching one student who was actively segregated from art activities at his early mainstream schools, despite having reasonable eyesight, and who continued to behave negatively during his art lessons no matter what method Harry used to communicate with this child. In the end, Harry found that he would only draw if he could use a computer, a method he had learned to rely on as a small child. His own computer was provided by the school to help with his requirements in literacy and numeracy, but although he became adept at using the class computer to create works of art in Harry's class, this student would still refuse to carry out tasks with traditional drawing equipment after perfecting his designs. Harry explained that he had become dependent on his computer too much to attempt these manual exercises and, consequently, he was barred from entering national art examinations. This was Harry's initial description of this student's work:

> INTERVIEWER: You remember we were talking earlier about students who'd come in from mainstream schools, integrated school?
>
> HARRY: Yes.
>
> INTERVIEWER: And the work they'd done, have you got anything by them...

HARRY: [He shows me some computer graphics designed by a lad who is partially sighted and began his education at mainstream school. Harry rates his sight at about 6/10 visual acuity. We were told he does all of his drawing on the class computer, but Harry has told me that he is struggling on the course and misbehaves.] He's got no drawing skills as such. He's got no formal drawing skills because he wasn't taught properly...

INTERVIEWER: Does he avoid drawing?

HARRY: ...He's got to do some drawing [for his coursework—we noted he cannot currently be entered for GCSE because he does not have traditional pencil or pen drawings.]

INTERVIEWER: But does he want to do it?

HARRY: No, he's not overly keen. He finds it hard. I mean he's done some nice work on the computer. I think I only got him because he came...I think he's really keen on computers, and so I think we'll see it go in that direction really. But he won't have a sketch book like my other students have got.

INTERVIEWER: And is that his choice?

HARRY: No, it's his because he doesn't do it. But rather than snarling up on that I've tried to find something that he can do. I mean, we only got him because when he arrived he chose to do art; because when he arrived he sort of tacked on to a group; and we were working in the library, when he came to see what the art group was doing; and we were actually on the computers that day; and he sort of said 'ooh yeah, art, I think I'll do art', you know, he chose to do it. (Harry, personal communication, April 2002)

Similarly, Taylor also described one student who was a high achiever, one that she had supported in his classes for several years before he eventually took art as a teenager. This student's art teacher appeared to be reluctant to set him the same or similar tasks as his sighted students, which, Taylor suggested, led the student to feel uncomfortable in these lessons and made him dread attending them. After this experience, when he was offered the chance to attend further art courses run by different teachers with a more positive outlook, he declined. The student felt after this period that he was not capable of art. This experience was very unfortunate, Taylor felt, as this student had initially picked this course because it sounded interesting and he had entered the class with an open mind. He appeared to have no previous bad experiences of learning that would suggest that he should doubt his potential to achieve as much as he had done in other, similar classes if he had wanted to.

In this particular case, I conjectured that Taylor's student was also put off by the context of drawing in art classes, but not necessarily the task of drawing itself. For instance, some time after his experiences in the art class. Taylor told me this student was given the same drawing tasks as his sighted peers during a math course—on this occasion he was taught how to draw perspective and two-dimensional objects to scale. Given this set of circumstances, he was able to pick up this skill with ease, as his teachers' support and positive expectations of him in this class gave him the necessary confidence to believe that such representations were achievable, and he could prove a sense of self-worth. What follows is an excerpt from Taylor's description of this student which illustrates this point:

> TAYLOR: ...I had a teacher who said, 'no, there's nothing that I can provide for this child'...there's nothing that I can do short of sitting with them one-to-one with me...which is not the aim of a mainstream class...It was supposed to be an enlightenment class. It wasn't

supposed to be something that was led specifically by a stranger, an insider, or an outside teacher. And I was crushed.

There was one boy who, he was one of my more academically gifted students. And he said, 'I have no musical talents'. They had to do either a music or an art credit. And he had absolutely no talent for music, he had no background in an instrument, and he couldn't sing at all and so he was assigned to an art class. We were all prepared to go in...

We should have shopped by teacher rather than shopped by title [of the class]. Within a high school regime you can't always choose the period or the time that that teacher will be there. So he ended up being in a class that wasn't, wasn't great. And the teacher basically sat him in a corner and gave him some clay, and said, you know, 'work with this', and the rest of the class was doing something, they weren't even working with clay. They were doing drawing, they were doing a variety of things. And he was just stuck there. And he said, 'you know, I feel really stupid. Why can't I do something else?' It was so demeaning.

INTERVIEWER: Did he [change his mind about] art because of it...

TAYLOR: He went on to college...He went into computers. I don't know whether he, I doubt if he ever chose to take art class. In the following year...he went in and negotiated with the person who is in charge of the scheduling and he got the credit, but didn't have to take art. He did something alternative instead... (Taylor, personal communication, November 2003)

In other sections of their interviews, many of the teachers also described observing behaviour that could be interpreted as what is often described as learned helplessness (Arnold, 1997; Deci & Chandler, 1986); that is, students become reliant on teachers to do an element of work for them. I also found that an overly liberal, positive, segregationist approach towards students could have as damaging consequences as the negative, segregationist approach of other teachers.

For instance, a student that Taylor supported was educated away from mainstream students by an untrained teacher in one school. Taylor found, however, that unlike her previous experiences of such teaching, this student's extraction from lessons was overcompensated for by his teacher, who told him he could achieve any art tasks sighted students could without any additional assistance and, during art lessons, would not criticise his work in any way or remove marks from his assessment, even when he made obvious mistakes. Instead, she often appeared to complement the student's mistakes and, it was Taylor's opinion, reduced his ability to detect any errors in his work. As a result, the student developed a highly complacent attitude to the quality of his work.

Eventually, Taylor found that although in the short-term the student wanted to attempt art projects with gusto, in the long-term his expectations were not fulfilled, and his understanding of what was successful and unsuccessful became highly ambiguous. This student's unrealistic expectations continued when he chose to apply for a place at a high school specialising in art.[1] Unfortunately, although he had help in building a portfolio for his interview, he continued to assume his limited paintings and drawings would be enough to secure him a place at the school. It was not only his technique that seemed naïve, it was also that his choice of subjects in his drawings and paintings seemed particularly limited, based as they were on simple representations of well-known cartoon characters, rather than the more traditional still life representations that were acceptable as portfolio entries at interview. As a result, he was rejected during the first stages of auditions for the high school, which left him despondent and unmotivated in his remaining art classes. What follows is an excerpt from Taylor's description of this episode:

> TAYLOR: I had a student; he had an inflated idea of his art ability...
>
> INTERVIEWER: By the teacher?
>
> TAYLOR: Well, he'd been in a self-contained class and well, he had some art talent, but I don't think, he didn't seem to have as much as he thought he had. But because he was head and shoulders, and he thought he was probably the brightest and probably the most academically able child, in his group [of students with disabilities]...but his art teacher was always "oh that's so wonderful", and compared to a kid in a regular class it wouldn't have made it.
>
> And I was with the year that, in [Ashton Gate] at the end of 8th grade, or at the end of the 8th year [around the age of 16] you apply to a high school. And he had decided he wanted to go to one of the art and design...schools,[2] which required an audition, as well as a portfolio. So early in the year when he had identified this desire, we tried to get him working... And, poor guy, his art teacher was willing to help and tried to help. He didn't quite get that he wasn't quite just going to be put into this school. He didn't realise it was really competitive and they weren't going to say "oh, he's a little blind kid we'll let him go in anyway", it was all on his merit.
>
> And he made some drawings; and got a portfolio; and it was missing a lot of the things it was supposed to have...and there was something there to

work with but not, not what would get him into the school. And he went to the audition where they were put in front of a drawing board, and given a task and had to draw two or three different things and he was just crushed. He came back and was demoralised. And his drawings after that seemed to get a little more [angry]. Not that he'd had a bad art experience, but he was led to believe something that wasn't…

Are we doing them a service by telling them that it's great work. Yes, but encourage but try not to pump them up too much or else…It wasn't realistic on his part, and it wasn't because he was blind but because he wasn't good enough… (Taylor, personal communication, November 2003)

I now conclude these findings, before presenting the conclusion to this book in the final chapter.

Conclusion

My observations and interviews in this second study demonstrated that there are definable patterns in the behaviour of a broad range of students in different social and educational contexts that relate to the early exclusion of blind students in art lessons. These teachers' experiences also demonstrate that exclusion can take the form of both underestimating students' abilities and ignoring their disabilities, to the cost of their full inclusion in lesson tasks and integrated environments. Therefore, I have found through these experiences that there is evidence of a lack of uniformity in understanding blind students' needs and capabilities in earlier mainstream art lessons, often caused by a lack of training or experience on the teachers' part. And as a consequence, this often contributes to later rejection of the subject.

Furthermore these observations and interviews also raised further questions about the wisdom of explaining behaviour in classroom environments by simply observing students and lessons *in situ*. In particular, these descriptions demonstrated a common understanding of many blind students' needs to redefine and renegotiate their art tasks in order to reduce their risks, even when it came at the expense of a development of their self-worth and obfuscated the development of their confidence.

For instance, Harry's student completed his drawings by using a computer package, preferring to renegotiate tasks when they became too difficult, even those that he knew were vital for his examination, in a manner that made their subject *more ambiguous* and relatively meaningless. This element of students' behaviour, therefore, would appear to contradict the mainstream argument, described at the beginning of this book, that inexperienced students are more likely to try and make exercises less ambiguous in order to reduce its risk of failure (Doyle 1979, 1983).

Finally, as I did in the previous chapter, these teachers noticed that there were noticeable disparities in the behaviour of students in the same class even when they had similar quantities of experience. This leads me to question the validity of the observation that behaviour is determined chiefly by the classroom environment, the nature of tasks within time, and the amount of students' experience, as I described in the first chapter. The fact that I was told of such extreme differences in individual classrooms by such an array of teachers means that this notion is far more complex and subtle than I had previously thought. In particular, the personal histories of blind people and the powerful social and cultural attitudes towards blindness, which were left unchecked by additional teacher training, needed particular scrutiny, as these factors had a significant effect on behaviour.

The following and final chapter of this book concludes my studies by discussing my original research hypotheses and questions.

ENDNOTES

1. In the United States, this is expected to be the first step towards applying for a course in a degree-awarding art college.
2. These schools are designed to take students who have the potential to go on to take art degrees.

Section IV

Addressing the Hypotheses

Chapter 7

Conclusion

> The tradition of all the dead generations weighs like a nightmare on the brains of the living.
> —K. Marx, *The Eighteenth Brumaire of Louis Bonaparte* (1937)

Introduction

This chapter concludes the studies I discussed in the previous chapters and explores the hypothesis and questions introduced at the beginning of this book. My objectives for this chapter are to discuss areas of my knowledge in which a cultural approach to disability can be applied, in order to further knowledge of the social aspects of blindness, and subsequently to provide suggestions for future practice, research, and above all social change. In order to achieve this, my conclusion is split into two segments. The first of these examines my hypothesis, and the second discusses the questions that were given in the introduction.

THE BOOK'S HYPOTHESIS

My hypothesis not only addressed the fundamental nature of attitudes towards blindness, but also addressed the fundamental nature of social and cultural myths that are taken for granted about blind students. More importantly, when I formulated this hypothesis, I wanted it to address the nature of the role of history and, more importantly, personal histories of students and their role in behaviour, confidence, and self-worth, which I found were the constituent ingredients of understanding and creating in the visual arts.

Attitudes towards students who are blind in the visual arts radically changed after they were integrated into mainstream schools, and this made students educated after this period, in general, more willing to undertake new art tasks. However, where attitudes have negatively affected the experiences of students who are blind in the visual arts, they have also affected their behaviour in art classes.

The evidence I uncovered in my studies did not generally support the first sentence of this hypothesis. In particular, I discovered in the course of my academic passage that such a broad statement about any form of disability became more and more difficult to judge. Moreover, the evidence I uncovered established that integration in art lessons was certainly not uniform after students were integrated into mainstreams classes, but was impossible to classify before this process, even though the rhetoric of many of these *progressive* schools attempted to convince the populous that it was (Hayhoe, 2008).

Even when I considered the alternatives, the evidence of this explanation was not compelling, and I had to concede that there were too many variables to consider saying that teachers' attitudes necessarily emanated from broader social and cultural attitudes to blind people. Moreover, in assessing this hypothesis, I felt it was important to test my evidence against the possible explanations that related to the students' blindness as a cause of *educational concern*. For instance, the mixed experiences in mainstream schools I discovered could be explained by the pressure on art teachers from their own professional expectations and performance management targets. Consequently, their attitudes to blind students would remain based on often uninformed opinions about competition in education culture, and especially in the broader economic setting of mainstream schools.

I could, however, support the second sentence in this hypothesis. In particular, all of the students that I observed who had suffered harmful experiences during art tasks in their mainstream schooling, whether this was in a mainstream institution or a school for the blind, *always* became evasive when they were presented with the same or similar tasks later. Distinctly similar observations were also made by the experienced art teachers I interviewed in England and the United States. Above all, the evidence I gathered at New College and Leicester University showed that there was no single cause and effect between teaching and students' sense of self-worth.

The confidence that these students developed and their personal histories, however, did form a clearly defined pattern of behaviour that determined their academic success in the visual arts later on in their lives. For instance, although these students experienced similarly positive expectations when they reached New College some 5 or 6 years previously, Anna and Emile often behaved in a way that belied mainstream experiences during their A-level projects. Of the two, only Anna had generally positive experiences during her art classes with her sighted peers. Emile, on the other hand, remembered mainly negative incidents in his mainstream projects, such as drawing with almost ridiculously large crayons or the humiliation of being given intellectually inferior tasks compared to the tasks of his sighted peers. Consequently, he avoided tasks that Anna would happily attempt to take risks with—even when it went beyond what she had to achieve in her A-level examinations, or when he knew that his avoidance ultimately risked failure and his academic future.

Furthermore, evidence I examined in both of my studies strongly suggested that the behaviour of students could also relate directly to the positive and negative qualities of experiences at the earliest ages of learning. In particular, students took more risks in art tasks in which they had positive experiences in their youngest years and avoided art tasks which had provided bad experiences during the same period.

In terms of my original comparison of Doyle's classroom observations and my own, therefore, my evidence questioned his supposition that classroom behaviour is always based on the quantity rather than the quality of experience. Nowhere was this more apparent than in my observation of Linda's avoidance of any challenging forms of sculpture or intellectual debate on this issue, despite her years of study at the studio. This was also apparent in Emile's avoidance of drawing and writing tasks he had been exposed to since early childhood, even in the subjects he adored and whose other tasks had brought him a sense of self-worth, such as sculpting and clay work.

There are, admittedly, further potential explanations for such behaviour that I had to consider. For example, Emile's behaviour in certain clay modelling tasks could challenge this interpretation. One alternative is that Emile was looking for a task in which he could gain self-esteem and confidence at New College as a blind student, as he lacked this in other academic subjects that relied more on sight, such as drawing and reading. Thus, he could have found clay particularly accessible as a tactile medium, and used it constantly as a tactile substitute for illustrating figurative representations. Evidence from his interview suggested that he used clay in Bas relief as he found he did not have to represent a set of faces with a high degree of visual similarity. In this, he would have had enough emotional intelligence to realise that this reduced the risk of making an artwork he knew could prove embarrassing because of his blindness.

However, this conjecture was very unlikely. In particular, Emile also found that he enjoyed photography at New College, and he worked with subjects such as mathematics and visually intricate elements of clay work, such as coloured glazes, that relied far more on his remaining vision than any of his other senses. He also conducted a great deal of research using a computer and shunned the Braille reading and writing technologies he had access to at New College. Thus, it did not seem that the physical elements of his blindness had a great effect on his sense of self-worth, his confidence, and above all his educational choices.

What now follows is an examination of my two questions.

THE BOOK'S QUESTIONS

My questions queried the fundamental nature of education and blindness, and also issues which related to all disabilities discussed in chapter 2. They also addressed the effect of the social attitudes to the visual arts and the blind, and the purposes and intentions of schools for the blind. It is the evidence raised in these questions that I now discuss.

(1) Can attitudes towards blindness in art education merely be discussed in terms of a physical disability, or are they affected by social and cultural assumptions?

This question was the study's initial motivation, and represents the main focus of this book. Evidence from both of the studies suggested that blindness was first and foremost a physical condition that often changed the way in which our students behaved and chose their art tasks. Furthermore, what I found in my descriptions suggested that their blindness often seemed responsible for their choices of subjects, techniques and even the media that they used. In particular, the students needed different apparatuses and teaching styles to *understand* the nature of aesthetics, no matter how capable they were. For instance, given assistance, Anna developed methods by which she could understand colours by their names and uses, and then developed her own methods of using analogies with tones to use these colours in her drawings. Consequently, she excelled in her A-level coursework and, by emphasising a greater tonal appreciation, developed her own monochrome photography project.

However, it has to be mentioned that in many instances the physical nature of the students' blindness did not disable them at all, psychologically or socially, and in several cases provided an incentive to pursue art tasks over academic ones. For instance, Emile concentrated on elements of his coursework, such as clay moulding and working on a potter's wheel, because he found that he could undertake these exercises easily and that his blindness caused him only occasional practical difficulties. In addition, his concentration on A-level art allowed him to pursue a subject that allowed him an experience of academic success. It also permitted him to avoid subjects that required large amounts of reading and writing, as his earlier mainstream school appeared to have excluded him from these tasks when younger.

Based on this evidence, blindness was not so much a physical dysfunction, as students demonstrated that their blindness could be managed comfortably with only slight adaptation and often significant success. There are, though, further considerations that complicate this issue. Based on the evidence in both of my studies, social and cultural attitudes towards these students' physical conditions and the resulting perception of its influence on their state of mind led to a socially objective disability. Most markedly, this was an observation that surfaced time and again in the interviews I held with art teachers, when it was felt that their students' behaviour also adapted in reaction to the beliefs of their early mainstream teachers. Hugo's and Emile's negative experiences of music and drawing also illustrated this difference in the main.

For instance, although it later transpired that Emile was capable of working easily with clay and photography (to speak of only a few of his art skills), his early mainstream art teachers excluded him from normal art exercises and did not provide him with the assistance that may have helped him overcome his physical disability. Consequently he lost confidence in art tasks that he had negative experiences of when he was younger. In this way, the tasks that he concentrated on during his A-level coursework were an escape from those in which he felt less confident, which provided him with a sense of self-worth beyond his long-term goal of an academic career.

This conclusion also supports the need for models of researching disability that include social, cultural, and physical elements, and not just individual elements of behaviour. In particular, the evidence presented in my case studies caused me to reappraise the evidence that I described in the publication of my first study's behavioural investigation of blindness and visual arts (Hayhoe, 1995, 2000).

This chapter now continues by addressing my second research question.

(2) What does blindness stop people from doing in the visual arts?

The short answer to this is apparently little, given access to the correct technologies and teaching. Furthermore, according to the evidence, the need for specific technologies and techniques can only be determined on an individual basis. In addition, the evidence clearly suggested that when appropriate techniques and technologies were selected, the self-belief of the students was enhanced, and they felt more capable of related tasks in the future.

For instance, despite her total colour blindness, Anna was able to understand labels on her coloured pencils, which provided a symbolic analogy to the colours she used. She was also taught that with a positive motivation she was capable of these and similar art tasks, even though initially her visual condition suggested otherwise. As a result, Anna found it relatively easy to conform to the academic demands of understanding colour.

Evidence from both of my studies has shown that it is possible that forms of blindness can provide physical and technological advantages in certain educational contexts. For instance, during her black and white photography project, Anna found it easier to work on her prints under infrared light than students with greater levels of sight. This finding confirmed Sack's (2003) study of genetically isolated colour blind islanders in the South Pacific, who found it easier to see at twilight than people with full sight.

This finding adds an extra dimension to what we understand by the phrase "normal" in art tasks. In particular, it highlights the inefficient and often obsequious way that the concept of identifying and classifying people according to their individual traits derives from the way that blindness has been regarded by science, philosophy, charitable foundations, governments, and educational administrators. Therefore, the students not only had to contend with difficulties presented from their actual blindness, but also the construction of knowledge about their abilities, classified according to this single physical trait.

This problem was a form of an *a priori* understanding of disability (Hayhoe, 2005), one in which socially acceptable assumptions were moulded into knowledge and were accepted by a broader culture. As a result, systems of education have evolved into social and cultural contexts of supposed normality, where students who are blind are in a vulnerable position before they begin learning. Thus, objective disabilities are created by knowledge systems themselves, even though such systems say they are designed to study and alleviate such physical and social traits.

Even in 20th-century studies of visual arts and blindness, von Senden and Revesz (1950) felt that people who were born blind or who acquired blindness early in life could not understand the beauty of art, as it held some higher metaphysical meaning that could only be extracted by the eyes. This exclusion came in the same era that potential was being recognised in art classes in Austria initiated by Viktor Lowenfeld (Hayhoe, 2008), under other cultural and social settings. Therefore, one issue that this question raised, and I hope I have risen more than any other in this book, is that there needs to be a greater emphasis on the subjective measure of disability than the objective. It is only through this form of consideration that we can really understand the potential of individuals rather than manage groups of people with disabilities, which is what we are simply working to achieve at the moment.

AND SO, WHERE NEXT?

This book has addressed many questions for future research and debate, as well as teaching practice and those in the position of policy making in the arts, although I feel it has merely scratched the surface of what I hope can be achieved. And so, where should these thinkers and practitioners go next? Over the course of 10 years or so of research, I have noticed that the main problem with the study of disability is the ghettoisation of enquiry. For instance, researchers in this field approach individual disabilities by perceptual, physical, or intellectual traits, such as the many psychologists who relentlessly pursue individual facets of blindness, often for the convenience of the research process, as a form of metaphor for understanding perception as a whole. Or they pursue the oversimplification of studies, which see all disabled people as a homogenous group to be patronised by political activists, social scientists, and social theorists for the ease of recommending social policy or defining procedures.

Although a great deal of interesting writing and thought has arisen from these studies, not least those I have discussed in this book, this approach has polarised notions of disability and impairment in much the same manner that similar approaches have polarised and oversimplified notions of so-called race and gender. Therefore, what is needed in future is a philosophical overhaul of thinking on this subject and a defining of the approaches to the ways we choose to involve people with disabilities, such as blindness and deafness; these are ways that those who oversee the visual arts, cultural integration, and education must play a vital part in.

REFERENCES

Abrahamson, M. (1983). *Social research methods*. New York: Prentice-Hall.

Albrecht, G., & Levy, J. (1981). Constructing disabilities as social problems. In G. Albrecht (Ed.), *Cross national rehabilitation policies: A sociological perspective* (pp. 11–33). London: Sage.

Arnold, N. G. (1997). *Learned helplessness and attribution for success and failure in LD students*. U.S. National Center for Learning Disabilities. Retrieved September 2005, from http://www.ldonline.or/ld_indepth/self_esteem/helplessness.html

Atkinson, P., & Hammersley, M. (1994). Ethnography and participant observation. In N. K. Denzin & Y. S. Lincoln (Eds.), *Strategies of qualitative inquiry* (pp. 110–136). Thousand Oaks, CA: Sage.

Barasch, M. (2001). *Blindness: The history of a mental image in Western thought*. London: Routledge.

Barnes, C., & Mercer, G. (2003). *Disability*. Cambridge, U.K.: Polity Press.

Bower, R. T., & Gasparis, P. (1978). *Ethics in social research: Protecting the interests of human subjects*. Wesport, CT: Praeger Publishers.

Burgess, R. (1985). The whole truth: Some ethical problems of research in a comprehensive school. In R. Burgess (Ed.), *Field methods in the study of education* (pp. 139–162). London: The Falmer Press.

Coakes, R. L., & Holmes-Sellors, P. J. (1992). *An outline of ophthalmology*. London: Butterworth-Heinemann.

Cresswell, J. W. (1994). *Research design: Qualitative and quantitative approaches*. London: Sage.

Deci, E., & Chandler, C. (1986). The importance of motivation for the future of the LD field. *Journal of Learning Disability, 19,* 587–594.

Department of Health. (2001, January). *Registered blind and partially sighted people year ending 31 March 2000, England*. London, HMSO.

Dharma Colwell, S. (1993). *The education of adults with disabilities*. Unpublished master's thesis, Bristol University, Bristol, U.K.

Doyle, W. (1979). Classroom tasks and students' abilities. In P. L. Peterson & H. J. Walberg (Eds.), *Research on teaching*. New York: McCutchan.

Doyle, W. (1983). Academic work. In N. S. Glasman & J. W. Pellegrino (Eds.), *Review of educational research* (pp. 159–199). Cambridge, MA: Longfellow Hall.

Foucault, M. (1989). *Madness and civilization* (R. Howard, Trans.). London: Routledge Classics.

Fougeyrollas, P., & Beauregard, L. (2001). Disability: An interactive person-environment social criterion. In G. L. Albrecht, K. D. Seelman, & M. Bury (Eds.), *Handbook of disability studies* (pp. 171–194). London: Sage.

French, S. (1994). Disabled people and professional practice. In S. French (Ed.), *On equal terms: Working with disabled people* (pp. 103–118). Oxford, U.K.: Butterworth-Heineman.

Freund, P. A. (1969). *Experimentation with human subjects.* New York: George Braziller, Inc.

Geertz, C. (1983). *Local knowledge: Further essays in interpretive anthropology.* London: Harper Collins/Basic Books.

Gleeson, B. (1999). *Geographies of disability.* London: Routledge.

Goffman, E. (1990). *Stigma: Notes on the management of spoiled identity.* London: Penguin.

Goffman, E. (1991). *Asylums.* London: Penguin.

Gramsci, A. (1971) *Selections from prison notebooks* (Q. Hoare, & G. Nowell Smith, Eds. & Trans.). London: Lawrence & Wishart.

Gregory, R. L. (1974). *Concepts and mechanisms of perception.* London: Duckworth.

Groce, N. E. (2001). *Everyone here spoke sign language: Hereditary deafness on Martha's Vineyard.* Cambridge, MA: Harvard University Press.

Hahn, H. (1985). Disability policy and the problem of discrimination. *The American Behavioural Scientist, 28*(3), 293–318.

Hahn, H. (1986). Public support for rehabilitation programmes: The analysis of U.S. disability policy. *Disability, Handicap, and Society, 1*(2), 121–137.

Hayhoe, S. (1995). *The art education of blind adults.* Unpublished master's thesis, Leicester University, British Isles.

Hayhoe, S. (2000). The effects of late arts education on adults with early visual disabilities. *Educational Research & Evaluation, 6*(3), 229–249.

Hayhoe, S. (2002, September). *The experience of children with visual impairments in visual arts education.* Paper presented at the International Conference on the Politics of Childhood, Hull University.

Hayhoe, S. (2003). The development of the research of the psychology of visual impairment in the visual arts. In E. Axel, & N. Levent (Eds.), *Art beyond sight* (pp. 84–95). New York: The American Foundation for the Blind.

Hayhoe, S. (2005). *An examination of social and cultural factors affecting art education in English schools for the blind.* Unpublished doctoral thesis, Birmingham University, Birmingham, U.K.

Hayhoe, S. (2008). *God, money, and politics: English attitudes to blindness and touch, from Enlightenment to integration.* Charlotte, NC: Information Age Publishing, Inc.

Hayhoe, S., & Rajab, A. (2000, September). *Ethical considerations of conducting ethnographic research in visually impaired communities.* Paper presented at The European Conference on Educational Research 2000, Edinburgh University.

Hitchcock, G., & Hughes, D. (1989). *Research and the teacher: A qualitative introduction to school-based research.* London: Routledge.

Hull, J. M. (2001). *In the beginning there was darkness.* London: SCM Press.

Jay, M. (1994). *Downcast eyes: The denigration of vision in twentieth-century French thought.* Berkley, CA: University of California Press.

Kelly, M. P. (2001). Disability and community: A sociological approach. In G. L. Albrecht, K. D. Seelman, & M. Bury (Eds.), *Handbook of disability studies* (pp. 396–411). London: Sage.

King, R. (1984). The man in the Wendy house: Researching infants' schools. In R. Burgess (Ed.), *The research process in educational settings: Ten case studies* (pp. 117–138). London: The Falmer Press.

Lowenfeld, B. (1981). Effects of blindness on the cognitive functioning of children. In Berthold Lowenfeld (Ed.), *On blindness and blind people* (pp. 67–78). New York: American Foundation for the Blind.

Merleau-Ponti, M. (2002). *Phenomenology of perception.* London: Routledge Classics.

Oliver, M. (1989). Disability and dependency: A creation of industrial societies. In L. Barton (Ed.), *Disability and dependency* (pp. 6–22). London: Falmer Press.

Paulson, W. R. (1987). *Enlightenment, romanticism, and the blind in France.* Princeton, NJ: Princeton University Press.

Pinar, W. F., Reynolds, W. M., Slattery, P., & Taubman, P. M. (2002). *Understanding curriculum. An introduction to the study of historical and contemporary curriculum discourses* (Vol. 17). New York: Peter Lang.

Pollard, A. (1987), *Children and their primary schools: A new perspective.* London: Falmer Press.

Sacks, O. (1993, May 10). To see and not to see: A neurologist's notebook. *The New Yorker*, 59–73.

Sacks, O. (1996). *The island of the colour-blind and Cycad Island.* London: Picador.

Sacks, O. (2003, July 28). The mind's eye: What the blind see. *The New Yorker*, 48–59.

Simons, H. (1989). Ethics of case study in educational research and evaluation. In R. Burgess (Ed.), *The ethics of educational research* (pp. 114–139). London: The Falmer Press.

Stangvik, G. (1998). Conflicting perspectives on learning disabilities. In C. Clark, A. Dyson, & A. Millward (Eds.), *Theorising special education* (pp. 137–155). London: Routledge.

Vygotsky, L. S. (1994). Principles of the social education of deaf and dumb children in Russia. In R. Van der Veer, & J. Valsiner (Eds.), *The Vygotsky reader* (pp. 19–26). Oxford, U.K.: Blackwell Publishers.

Wickham, C. (1988). *The development of provision of extra mural education for disabled adults.* Bristol, U.K.: Bristol University Press.

Williams, G. (2001). Theorising disability. In G. L. Albrecht, K. D. Seelman, & M. Bury (Eds.), *Handbook of disability studies* (pp. 123–144). London: Sage.

Williams, P. (1994). The Richard Attenborough Centre. Leicester University, Leicester, U.K.

WHO (World Health Organisation). (1989). *International classification of impairments, disabilities, and handicaps.* Geneva: Author.

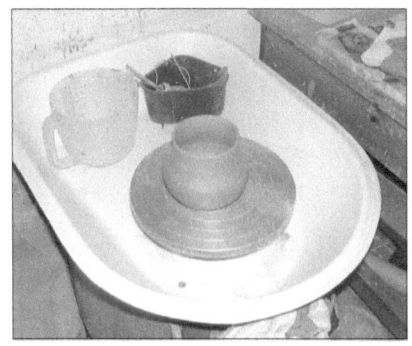
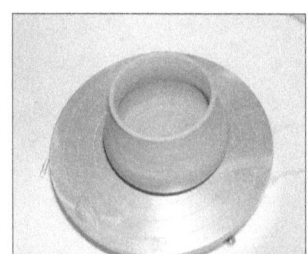
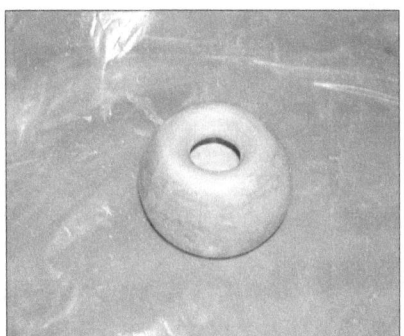

Emile's Racu pottery-making process in its early stages.

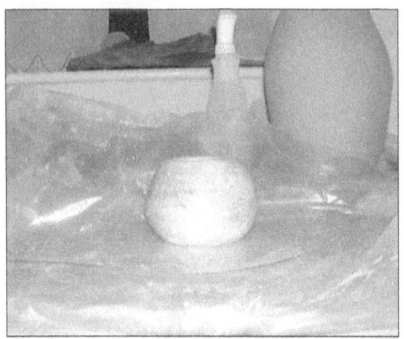
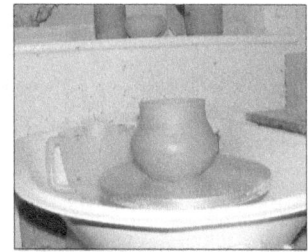

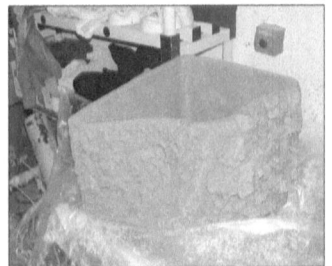

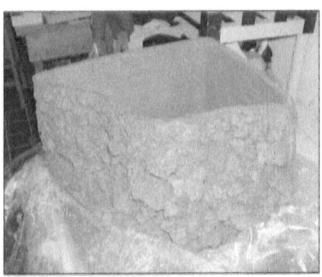

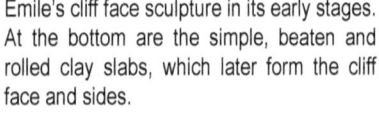

Emile's cliff face sculpture in its early stages. At the bottom are the simple, beaten and rolled clay slabs, which later form the cliff face and sides.

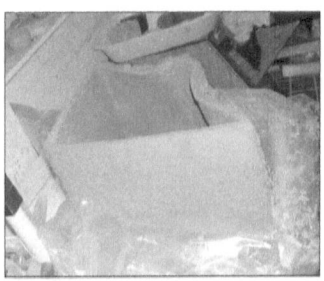

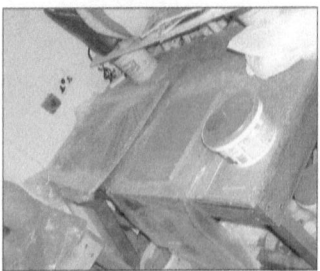

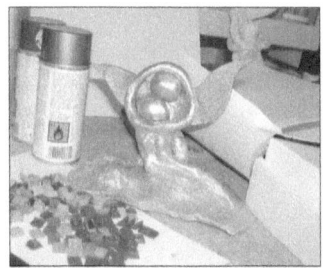

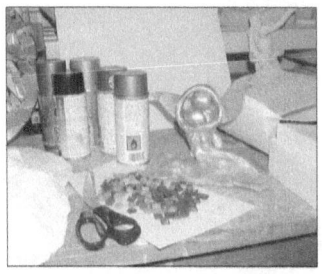

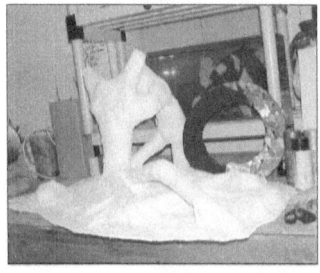

Anna's sculpture-creation process. The top two photographs show her maquettes of the finished piece. The third photograph shows her creation process with mud rock. The final photograph shows Anna's final experiments with wings in cardboard (*bottom*) on this and the following two pages.

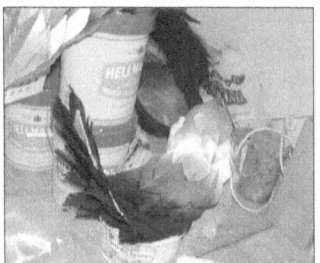

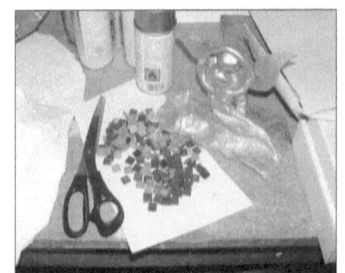
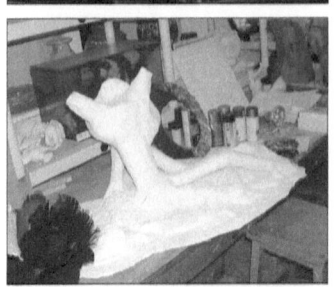
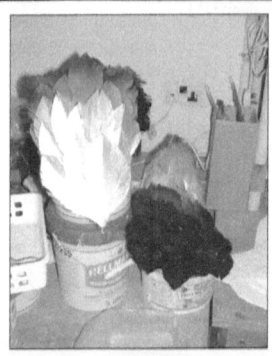
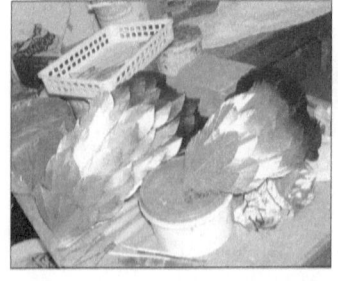

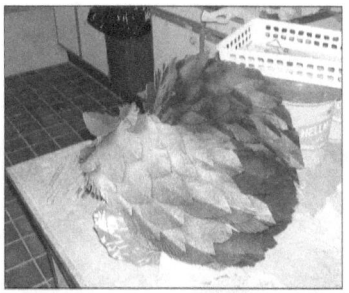
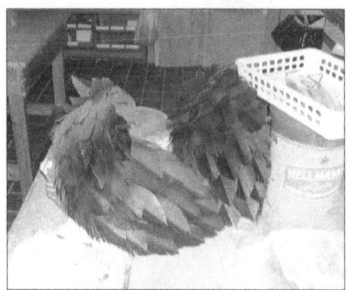
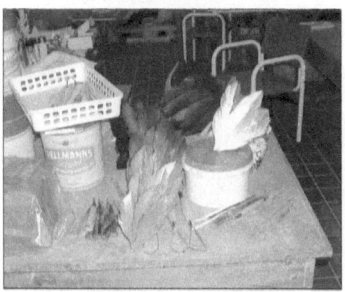

Anna's final experiments with wings (*continued*).

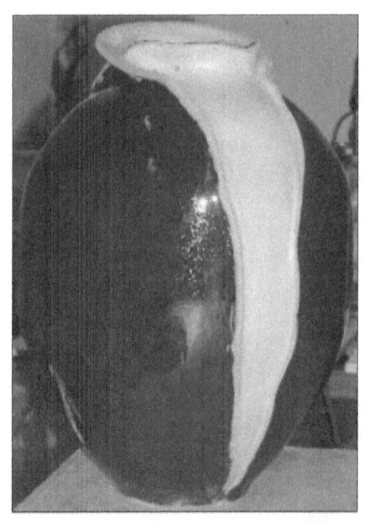

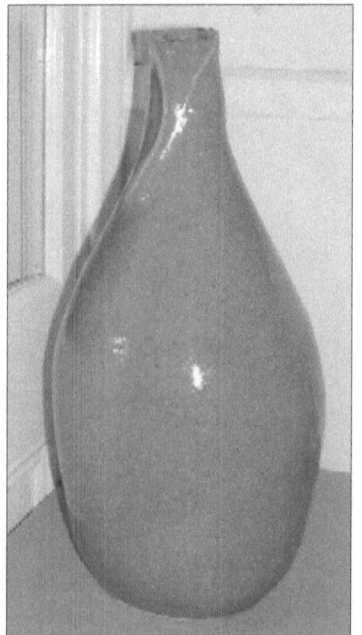

Emile's work prior to my observations. They are both cider jars that were the result of experimentation on the theme of seed pods.

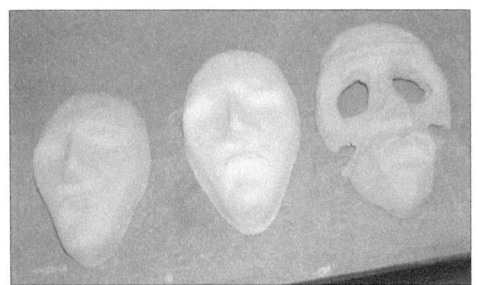

Emile's Mask Projects from a previous year's work.

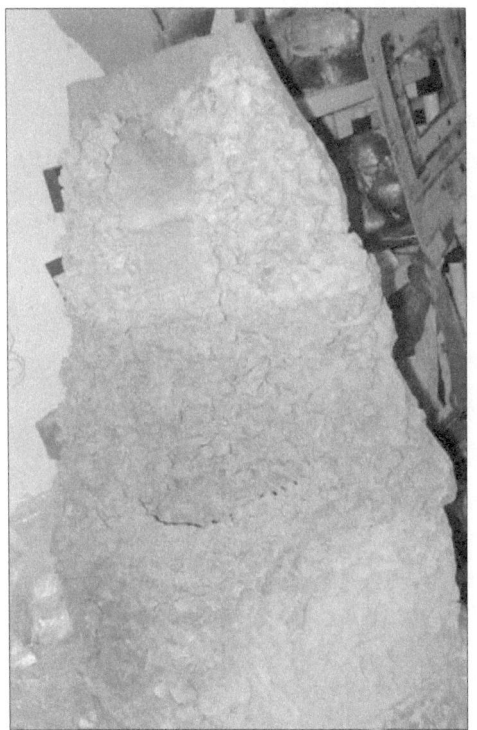

The front face of Emile's sculpture of a cliff face.

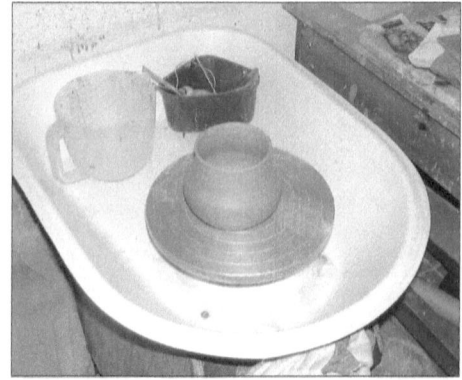

Photographs showing the development of Emile's Racu pottery (*top*) and the Back of his sculpted cliff face in his main project (*bottom*). It is clearly in three separate sections, and it is hollow inside.

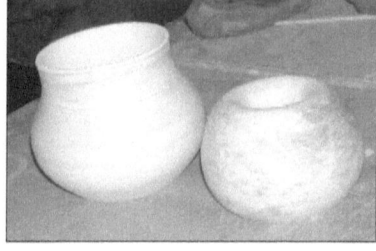

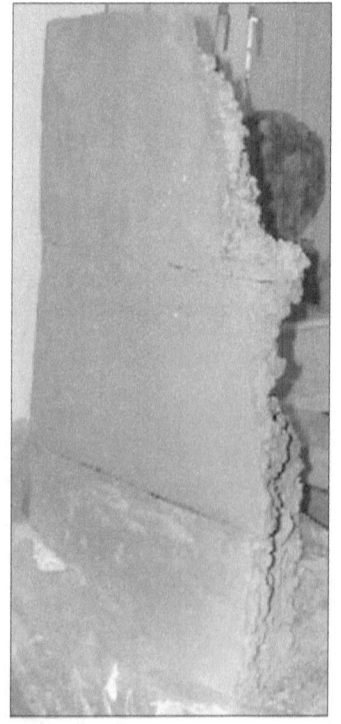

Various stages of pottery work by Emile: *left*, a completed pot from a previous project; *right*, semi-complete Racu pottery experimentations.

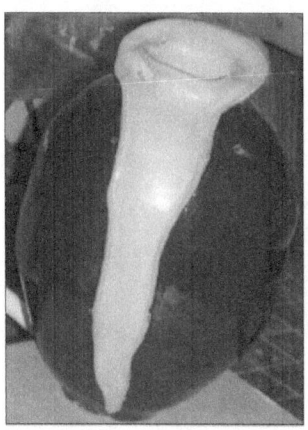
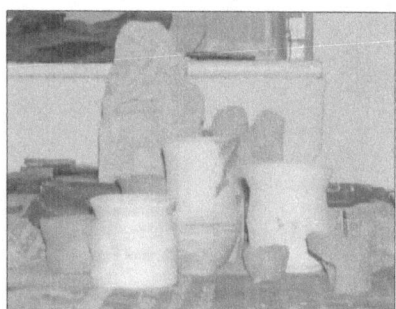

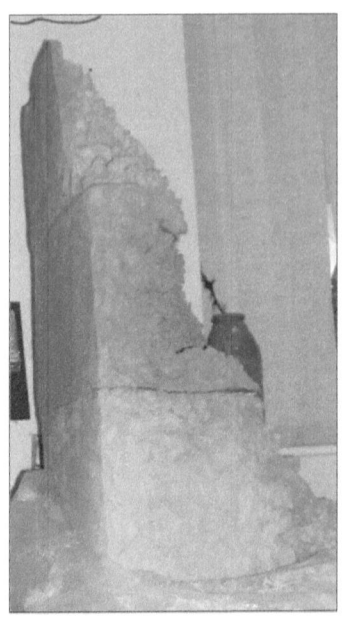 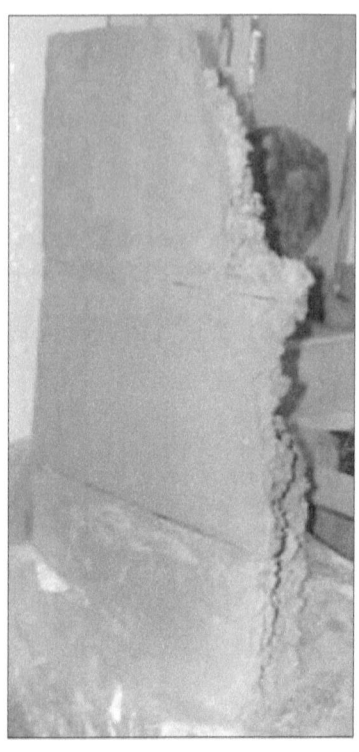

The back faces of Emile's sculpture in progress.

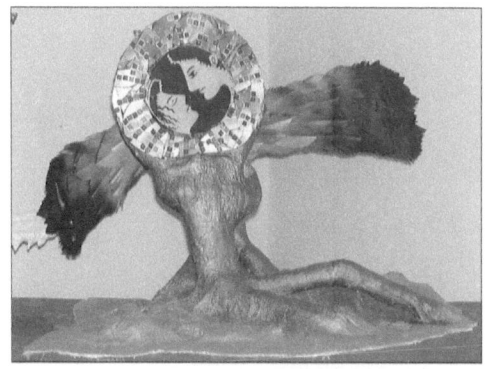

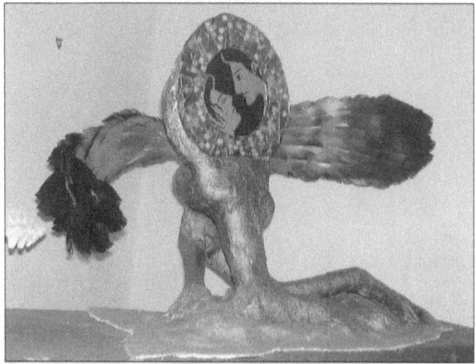

Four views of Anna's completed sculpture project—this and next page.

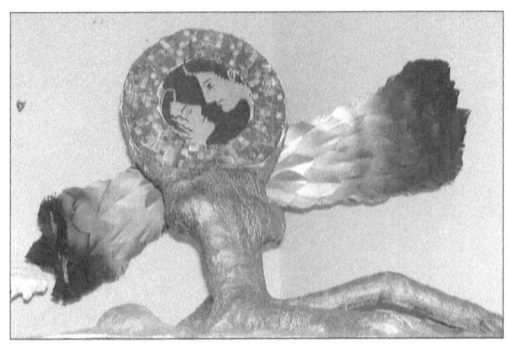

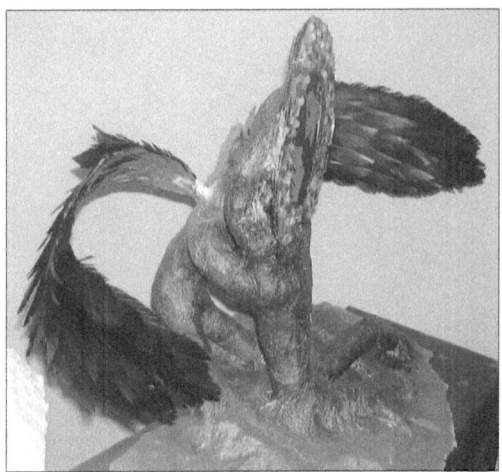

Four views of Anna's completed sculpture project (*continued*).

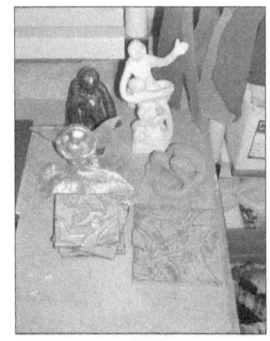

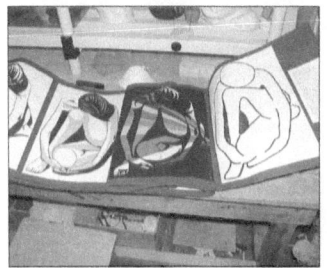

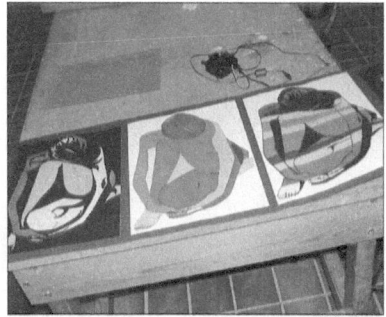

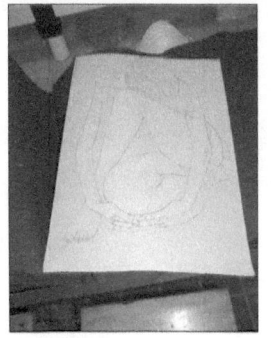

Anna's original drawings for her sculpture, with life figures, and some original experimentation with maquettes (*top left*)—on this page and following page.

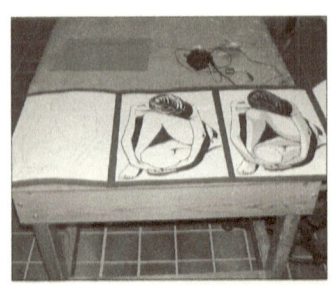
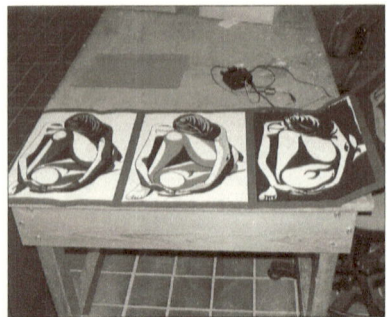
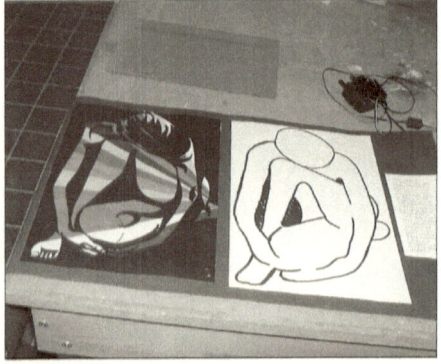

Anna's original drawings for her sculpture, with life figures, and some original experimentation with maquettes (*continued*).

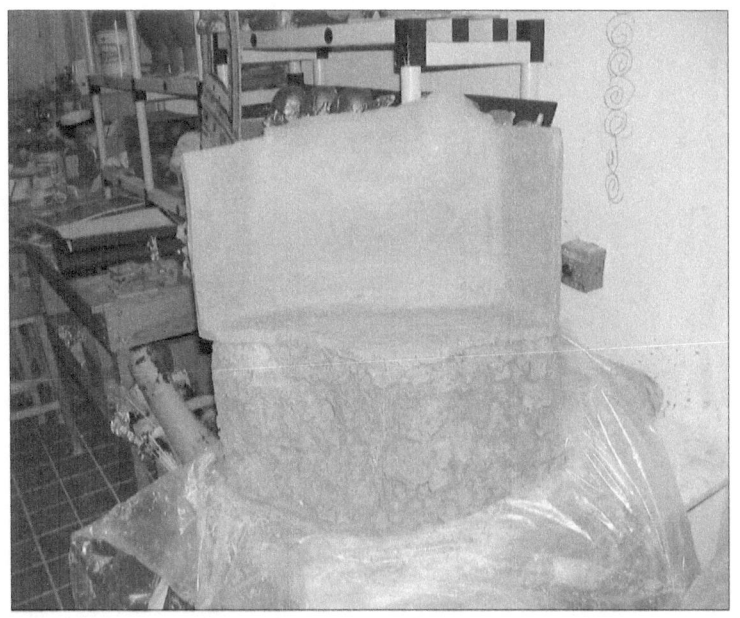

Emile's hollow cliff face sculpture in progress—this page and following page.

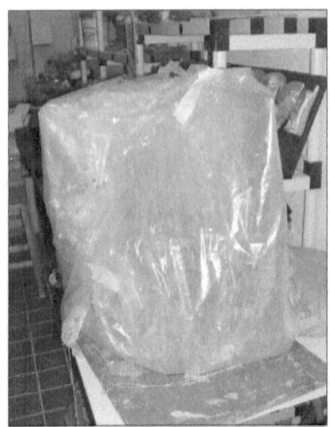

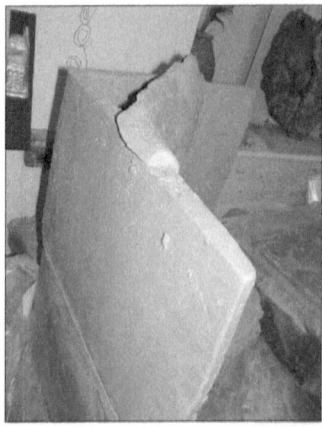

Emile's hollow cliff face sculpture in progress (*continued*).

INDEX

ability, 18, 26–27, 43, 48, 56, 63, 65, 118, 132–133, 144–146, 150–151
able bodied, 19, 40–42, 44
Abrahamson, M., 48
achromatism, 28–29
advanced level (A level), 14, 89, 109, 112–113, 117, 122–123, 130, 160, 162–163
Albrecht, G. & Levy, J., 38–39
ambiguity, 6–8, 12, 69, 84
Anna, 108, 120–133, 159–160, 162–164
antiquity, 35
Arnold, N. G., 9, 149
art, 4–5, 9–10, 12, 14–18, 22, 30, 44, 47–48, 50, 52, 55, 57–60, 62, 72–75, 81, 85–87, 93, 102–103, 107–133, 140–153, 158–165
Art Beyond Sight, 138
asylums, 31, 141
Atkinson, P., 48
avoidance, 8–9, 13, 84, 89, 101–102, 107, 115, 128, 131, 145, 160

Barasch, M., 35–36
Barnes, C., 37, 41
basket weaving, 50, 55
Beauregard, L., 41, 44

Bible, the, 35–37
blind culture, 139
blind, the, 4, 16, 36, 48, 52–54, 63, 75, 86, 116, 134, 139, 161–162
blindness, 4–5, 13, 16–18, 21–22, 27–30, 35–36, 48–49, 59, 64, 73, 108, 110, 120, 128–129, 142–143, 146, 153, 157–166
Bower, R. T., 48
Braille, 28, 53–54, 64, 161
Bristol, 6, 9, 47, 49, 66–69, 71–72, 86, 88, 101
Bristol University, 6, 49, 71, 86, 88
brittle bone disease, 49, 55
Burgess, R., 48

Casio keyboard, 52–54
Chandler, C., 9, 149
clay, 55–58, 65, 67, 112–119, 124, 129, 132, 149, 160–163
Coakes, R. L., 29, 59, 110
colour, 59, 61, 67, 110, 120–122, 128–129, 132–133, 164
colour blindness, 120–121, 128, 164
cone dystrophy, 120
confidence, 4
confine negotiation, 71–103

congenital blindness, 29
congenital optic nerve hyperplasia, 110
craft work, 60
Cresswell, J. W., 48

deafness, 33, 166
Deci, E., 9, 149
denial, 25, 43, 115
Department of Health, 30
depression, 22
Dharma Colwell, S., 65
disability, 4–5, 15, 17–19, 23–44, 55, 65, 75, 129, 131, 157–158, 162–163, 165–166
disease, 18, 27, 49, 55, 59, 110
Doyle, W., 6–8, 153
drama, 86, 109
drawing, 7, 111, 116–119, 121–124, 128, 132, 146–149, 152, 160, 163

early blindness, 29, 59
Emile, 108, 110–120, 131–132, 159–163
England, 14, 16, 30, 33, 47, 59, 70, 110, 134, 137–154, 159
ethics research, 139
European Social Fund (ESF), 54, 58
exclusion, 9–11, 32, 38, 40–41, 55, 131, 144, 152, 165
experimentation, 114, 124–125, 127, 133

Foucault, M., 31, 34–35, 38
Fougeyrollas, P., 41, 44

French attitudes to blindness, 35
French, S., 40–41, 44
Freund, P. A., 48

Gasparis, P., 48
GCSE, 109, 112, 122, 147
Geertz, C., 72
Gerard, 112–115, 117, 119, 126–129, 133–134, 141, 143–144
glasses, 20, 27–28, 77
glaucoma, 28, 59
Gleeson, B., 38
Goffman, E., 31–32, 34, 38
Gramsci, A., 40
Gregory, R. L., 22
Groce, N. E., 33

Hahn, H., 39
Hammersley, M., 48
handicap, 32, 42
Hayhoe, S., 6, 8, 11, 16, 29, 48, 63, 73, 77, 79, 81–83, 91–92, 95, 97, 99, 108, 113, 117–119, 126, 158, 164–165
Headmaster's Conference (HMC), 108
hearing problems, 73
Hitchcock, G., 48
Holmes Sellors, P. J., 29, 59, 110
Hughes, D., 48
Hugo, 49–58, 60, 62–65, 163
Hull, J. M., 36–37

images, 37, 67, 120, 126
impairment, 20, 24, 28–29, 38–39, 42, 127–128, 166

Index   191

integration, 4, 103, 134, 139–140, 144, 158, 166
interviewing, 33, 47

Jay, M., 35

Kelly, M. P., 41, 44
King, R., 48

ladies, the, 75–76, 78, 81–82, 84
late blindness, 30
legal integration, 140, 144
Leicester, 9, 47–49, 52, 55, 57, 66–67, 69, 72–74, 88, 101
Leicester University, 6, 48, 52, 54, 57, 62, 71, 73, 159
Lickey Grange School, 55
Linda, 73–86
literacy, 111, 116, 132, 146
lizard(s), 110, 113–114
Local Education Authority (LEA), 108, 135
Lowenfeld, B., 32
Lowenfeld, V., 165

macro study of disability, the, 15, 30–31, 33–39, 42–43
mainstream school(s), 4–5, 16, 75, 108, 110, 117, 120–121, 129, 138, 141, 146–147, 158–159, 163
maquettes, 113, 124, 129
Marx, K., 157
material culture, 40
memory, 7–8, 29, 61, 77
Mercer, G., 37, 41, 43
Merleau-Ponty, M., 25

micro theory of disability, the, 15, 30–33, 37, 43
music, 49–55, 61–62, 64, 73–74, 82, 86, 109, 145, 149, 163
myths, 3–4, 30, 35–36, 158

negotiated practice. *See* negotiation
negotiation, 8–9, 31, 38, 40, 43, 69, 71–103, 107, 119, 128, 131, 140, 149, 153
New College, Worcester, 59–60, 107–112, 117–121, 126, 129, 131, 133–134, 137–138, 140–141, 143, 159, 161

objective disability, 25–32, 35, 163
observations, 6, 8–9, 12–15, 17, 22, 37, 44, 47–49, 55, 63, 68–69, 72–73, 75–79, 81–83, 86, 89, 91–93, 95, 97, 99, 101–102, 107–108, 112, 115–119, 123, 126–128, 132–133, 137–138, 144–145, 152–153, 159–160, 163
Oliver, M., 40
opinion, 4, 7–8, 76, 99, 118, 159
osteogenesis imperfecta, 49
oxygen blindness, 49

painting, 59–63, 67, 90–91, 99–101, 111, 121, 150
participant observation, 112
Paulson, W. R., 35–36
perception, 22, 29, 59, 63, 110, 132, 166

peripheral vision, 29
photography, 110, 125–126, 130, 161–164
physical education (PE), 56
piano, 21, 49–56, 64
Pierre, 59–63
Pinar, W. F., 44
plastecine, 56
Pollard, A., 86
psychology, 34

Rajab, A., 48
Red Lodge, Bristol, 88, 90–100
Renaissance, 34–35
rhetoric, 30, 34, 36, 68–69, 84–86, 100–101, 158
Richard Attenborough Centre. *See* Richard Attenborough Centre for Disability and the Arts
Richard Attenborough Centre for Disability and the Arts, 48, 52–53, 62, 66, 74–75
risk, 6–9, 11–13, 68–69, 76–77, 79, 83–84, 88–91, 93, 95, 97, 99–101, 107–134, 153, 161
RNIB New College, Worcester. *See* New College, Worcester
routine, 7–8
Royal National College, 57
Royal National Institute for the Blind (RNIB), 57–58, 86, 108

Sacks, O., 22–23, 25, 29
schools for the blind, 4, 6, 15–16, 48, 63, 75, 86, 116, 134, 137, 140–142, 144, 146, 162

sculpture, 7, 52–53, 56–58, 61–62, 69, 72–74, 76, 78–79, 81, 84–85, 112–113, 117–119, 123–125, 127–128, 130, 160
segregation, 110, 144
self-esteem, 6–13, 66–67, 69, 72–73, 117–118, 130, 132–133, 161
self-worth, 4, 11–12, 73, 103, 108, 117, 120, 132–133, 140, 148, 158–161, 163
Sharon, 51, 55–60, 64–65
Simons, H., 48
soapstone, 73–74
social and cultural study of blindness, 15, 17–44
social and cultural study of disability. *See* social and cultural study of blindness
social model of disability, 24
Stangvik, G., 43
Steinbeck, J., 3
stigma, 32, 43
subjective disability, 25, 27–28
symbolic, 32, 164

task(s), 6–9, 11, 13, 18, 69, 91, 93, 118, 132–133, 148, 152, 161
touch, 28, 57, 59, 93, 99
trait(s), 18–19, 23, 26, 33, 43, 133, 165

United States (U.S.), 8, 107, 134, 137–154, 159

visual acuity, 27, 29, 110, 120, 147
visual impairment, 20, 28–29, 127–128
Vygotsky, L. S., 32, 38

weaving, 50, 55, 74
wheelchair, 20–21, 27, 49, 76
Wickham, C., 68
Williams, G., 38

Worcester, 55, 59–60, 107–111, 138
Worcester College for the Blind Sons of Gentlemen. *See* New College, Worcester
Worcestershire. *See* Worcester
World Health Organisation (WHO), 42

Yves, 72, 86–101

www.ingramcontent.com/pod-product-compliance
Lightning Source LLC
Chambersburg PA
CBHW020646220526
45464CB00001B/309